SEE LOVE

~

KNOW GOD

ALSO BY DAVID MONTGOMERY, M.D.

Loving to Heal: Easing the Way to Wellness

SEE LOVE

~

KNOW GOD

A Transformational Adventure Beyond Belief

David Montgomery, M.D.

David Montgomery, LLC

ISBN 979-8-9920738-2-9

This book is a work of fiction. Names, characters, businesses, organizations, places, events and incidents are the product of the author's imagination or used fictitiously. Any resemblance to actual persons, living or dead is entirely coincidental.

Cover photo ©Iryna Kushnarova, Dreamstime.com
ID: 347227229

Table of Contents

"What is Seen as Love
Is what unites, nourishes and transforms
Both the Seer and the Seen."
Love

Prelude

Saturday, June 8

This is a story of two precocious eleven-year-olds whose soul paths have woven through many lifetimes and now converge again on Saturday, June 8. Their tale unfolds through their eyes and the eyes of those souls whose lives they touch, all speaking as One voice to reveal what mere physical sight cannot see.

And so, it begins...

***

David Walden looks out the window to see kids gathering in the field up the street. He grabs his glove and races down the stairs, yelling to his mother that he is going out to play ball. He runs full-speed to get to the group before they finish dividing into teams. He is always the last to be picked on the rare occasions he was picked at all. David hopes today is going to be different.

Butch yells to him, "No need to hurry, shrimp, no one wants you on their team. Why don't you grow more first?"

David scans for anyone to support him. A few guys laugh in agreement with Butch, and others look away in silence.

"Give me a chance, I'm getting better," David pleads.

Butch turns to the group. "Anyone want to give the shrimp a chance?"

Steve says, "We've got our teams balanced, we don't need him."

Butch turns back to David. "See? We don't want you, so scram."

"Okay, but you don't have to be so mean about it."

"I wouldn't be mean if you weren't such a freak."

David turns around and mopes off, holding his glove over his face to hide the tears. He drops his glove on a patio table outside his house and runs into the woods. He looks for a big tree to climb, one that is far away enough that his mother won't see him. He is sure to get punished if she knows. Sitting in a tree soothes him, which is what he needs most right now.

David climbs trees, something many kids who reject him cannot or will not do. He always climbs higher than anyone else. Sometimes he would climb up one tree, and cross over to another one before climbing down. However, these skills never garner much respect from the boys in the neighborhood.

David finds the perfect tree and navigates his way up the branches of another smaller tree until he can reach a branch in the big tree. He climbs high, figuring the higher he goes, the closer to God he will be. He finds a comfortable perch about three-fourths of the way up. His breathing slows as he views the tops of smaller trees. Now he is ready to talk.

"Okay, God, why did you make me the way I am? I know I am still young and growing, but why do I have to be smaller than kids even younger than me? It makes me an easy target for bullies. I just don't understand. My mom has no answers for me. Did you make me small as punishment for something that I did wrong or am I just bad? If I'm not good enough for you how could anyone possibly like me? Is it because I haven't always told the truth or obeyed my mom? Or, maybe I'm bad for asking too many questions or because

2

I can't sit still in church. Do you think that I have been taken over by the devil? Sometimes I really hate my life. Can you help me?"

He lets a pause blanket the echo of his voice before going on. "I don't know why I talk to you; you never talk back. I bet you aren't even real. People just make up stories about you so they feel better about their life or to control other people. I have been told I should fear you because you are very powerful and can get furious if I don't obey your commandments. Mr. Rigid, my Sunday school teacher, told the class that as long as we believe in Jesus and repent our sins, you won't send us to burn in hell for eternity. Is that right? Does that mean that anyone who doesn't believe in Jesus as the savior will be automatically sent to hell? It seems kind of drastic for someone who is supposed to be loving. Whatever that means."

He lets the sounds of the forest take over for some minutes before continuing. "I'm getting pretty frustrated sitting here talking to myself. God, where are you? I want someone in my life who will be there for me and not try to hurt me if I made a mistake. My mom's the one I have to please. Her anger terrifies me. I hated when she sent me away to live with another family so she could work. Lucky for me it only lasted two school years."

I am glad I didn't have to be sent away after she married my stepdad. I'm not sure yet if he will stick around if I make him angry. Who can I trust? Who will accept me and be my friend? It can't be someone like you, God, because you won't talk to me. Maybe I need to learn how to please people better."

David climbs down the big tree, transfers to the smaller tree and continues low enough to jump to the ground. A moment later, he is surprised by a deer walking toward him. He stands very still as the deer approaches.

"How are you, deer? I am David." He reaches up and touches the deer's neck. The two stare into each other's eyes for a few moments before she turns around and wanders off into the woods. Even though the neighborhood kids rejected him and God wouldn't talk to him, the brief time with the deer has lifted his spirits.

He is still beaming when he enters the kitchen. "You look pretty happy," Mom says. "The ball game must have gone well."

"I didn't get to play. No one wanted me on their team. They wouldn't even give me a chance. They said I was too small. When am I going to grow? Do you know what it's like to not have friends?"

"I have seen you playing with other kids. Don't you think they are your friends?"

"I don't know if you have ever noticed or not, but I only play with others when I go to their house or search them out. They never come here asking for me to come and play with them. They play with me as a last resort."

"What did you do if you weren't playing ball?"

"I wanted to be by myself so I went into the woods to explore. I wanted to talk to God. I had some important questions but he was nowhere around."

"I hope you weren't climbing a tree."

"No Mom, I wasn't." David couldn't risk his mom being angry with him today. He quickly changes the subject. "I saw a deer and it let me pet its neck. It was really amazing."

"You must be careful around wild animals, David. You can never tell when they will try to hurt you."

"Sounds a lot like people," David replies. "I'm going up to my room."

David spends the rest of his afternoon playing video games and imagining himself as a superhero.

***

Angela is busy drawing when her grandmother enters her room. "I thought you might be more tired today after your chemotherapy yesterday," says Nana. "I just gave Sammy his lunch. Would you like something to eat?"

"No, Nana, I'm not very hungry."

"You've got to eat something to keep your energy up."

"Maybe I'll have some chocolate milk after I finish drawing. I had an image in my head and wanted to draw it. I'm almost done."

4

Nana looks at Angela's drawing and says, "You haven't drawn anything like this before. Can you tell me a story about your picture?"

"Sure. This is a boy sitting high in the tree. He is talking to God and is sad that God is not talking back to him. He wonders if there really is a God or not. I wonder the same thing. I keep asking God why I got cancer and he hasn't answered me yet. A deer is below looking up at the boy. I think she is the boy's friend. I'm going to draw another picture of the boy petting the deer."

"Who is this boy?" Nana asks.

"I don't know. He is just a boy. I wonder if I will meet him someday."

"You are really creative Angela. I enjoy seeing your imagination come to life in your drawings. I wish your momma could see your pictures. I know she would love them. "I wish she could see them too, Nana. I really miss her."

"I know, my child. I also miss her."

Chapter 1

Questions Without Answers

Sunday, June 9

"Come on, David, hurry up or you will be late for church," mom calls out.

"Do I really have to go, mom?"

"Of course, you do. Why wouldn't you want to go to Sunday school"

"I would rather stay home and play," David pleads. "We just sit around as the Sunday school teacher reads stories from the Bible. It doesn't mean anything to me. It's so boring, plus the teacher gets upset with me when I ask questions that he doesn't know the answers to."

"It is important, honey, that you learn about God and Jesus so that you can live your life with meaning and purpose."

"What does David slaying Goliath have to do with the meaning and purpose of my life?"

"David, we don't have time to talk about this. Your dad and Michael are already waiting in the car. You will go to church!"

Michael is David's older brother, who is eighteen and will be going into the Navy in a few months.

"Okay." David saunters to the car with his head down. The ride to church is long enough for him to renew his anger with his parents for making him go to church and with God for making him the way he is. He keeps his feelings locked behind tightened lips and creased eyebrows.

Entering the classroom, David spies his favorite seat by the window and rushes to grab it. The church is in a different neighborhood and school district than where David lives. The kids are friends or at least know each other. Their chairs are pulled close to each other. David is sitting too far to hear what they are laughing about. He hopes whatever it is, it isn't about him.

David thinks he is like a piece of a puzzle put in the wrong box. This is not a new feeling for him. From the time he started school at 5 years old, he often found himself alone on the playground, longing for acceptance. His fear of rejection told him it was safer this way. He tried to connect with the other kids one Valentine Day at school by making cards for each of them. He put one in every bag taped to the back of each desk chair. He tried but couldn't hold back the tears when he found his own bag empty.

Mr. Joseph Rigid, the Sunday school teacher, comes in and says he is going to read from the bible. It doesn't take long for David to zone out. He looks out the window and dreams of being outside. He notices a bird flying by and wishes he could fly. He would up to top of the tallest tree.

"David! David, are you listening to me," Mr. Rigid barks.

David turns toward the teacher. "What?"

"Why aren't you paying attention to what I'm reading?"

"To be honest, I'm not interested," David replies. "This seems like work to me, Mr. Rigid. I thought we shouldn't have to work on Sunday."

"David, you are being very disrespectful to me and God."

"I'm sorry, I told you the truth. I suppose I could have apologized or told you I have ADHD. I certainly didn't mean to be disrespectful to you and especially God, if he exists. I'm not really sure what you say about God is really true. I find it hard to believe in something that I can't see or someone who won't speak to me."

"David, you have to have faith that what I'm telling you is true."

"Why? Why is what you say about Jesus more right than what my Jewish friend George says? Even the Baptists and Catholics have different rules and beliefs and they are Christians. And what about Buddhists, and Muslims, they all want everyone to have faith that what they believe is right. I would like to hear from God personally. I would ask him what is right. You tell me that God listens to my prayers. Well, I have been praying, asking God to talk to me. I have important questions, and he hasn't bothered to say one word to me."

"David, it doesn't work that way. God won't speak to you directly," says Mr. Rigid.

"Didn't he talk to Moses, Jesus, and some others? Didn't he appear to Isaiah?" David says.

"Yes, but those were exceptional circumstances."

"You tell me that God almighty is the creator of everything; who listens to the prayers of everyone but he isn't so powerful that he can find a way to answer them? Or maybe he has been speaking to people all along but no one is listening, or they don't think it is really God speaking."

"That's enough David. I want to continue with the lesson today."

This isn't the first time David has irritated others with his questions. David begins to pray in silence. "God, if you really exist, I hope you weren't upset with me. I would really like to learn the Truth about you and not rely on faith that the adults say I should have. I know I've asked many times but please talk to me." Then he goes back to daydreaming until Sunday school is over.

Next, he has to endure the main church service with no windows to look out. He must sit on a hard bench and listen to the minister give a lecture about something he isn't interested in. David wishes he could sit in the back of the balcony with Michael and his friends. Drifting off into his dream world without being noticed would be easier. But Dad wanted David to sit close to the front of the church with him. Dad often gives David a peppermint candy midway through the service, but today, David gets two candies. David keeps one and passes the other one to the college guy who has been coughing next to him all through the service. The guy smiles and nods thanks.

David always gets nervous peeling the wrapper off the candy. He is sure the congregation can hear the crackling sound of the cellophane. Today is great because he waits and unwraps it when the older guy starts coughing. It is hard for David to sit still for the whole service. At some point he starts squirming and it triggers 'the look' from his father. That usually works temporarily but some Sundays he gets two or three of those *looks* and dad's hand gently touching the top of his leg before he settles down.

***

Nana was a faithful churchgoer before she took custody of Angela and Sammy. Angela receives her chemotherapy on the weekdays and recovers on the weekends. She doesn't think it is right to leave Angela at home by herself while she is still sick from the medications. Nana sometimes watches televised church services. They are never the same as being there in person. She isn't interested in the message they preach as the energy of being surrounded by friends caring for each other. Church is a break from her daily stresses. It offers her a time to appreciate God and life. She enjoys singing in the choir, and that joy stays with her the rest of the day. Nana tells Angela and Sammy about God's love and the importance of prayer. Angela listens to Nana while silently questioning the truth of what Nana says about God's love.

Why would a loving God make my life so miserable?

Nana enters Angela's room and finds her sitting in bed with her drawing pad. "Do you want to come down and get something to eat? I'm concerned you are not getting enough to eat or drink. You are still losing weight."

10

"Maybe later, Nana. My stomach is still upset and I have a headache."

"You hardly ever have a headache. I'll get you some Tylenol."

"I am not recovering as fast as I used to. I sleep, dream, wake up, draw and then fall asleep again."

"What are you drawing today?"

"It's the same boy as yesterday. He is sitting by a window looking out. I don't think he wants to be where he is."

***

On the way home, David's dad said, "Mr. Rigid talked to me about your behavior during Sunday school today. He said you were distracted and when he asked you to pay attention, you said you were not interested in the lesson. You then went on to question even the existence of God. Is that true?"

David looks down and says, "Yes, that is true. Do you want me to accept things adults tell me as true just because they are adults? I want to know why God can't tell me himself."

"David, I can't answer that question and I can't speak for God."

"Isn't that just what you are doing when you spout passages of the Bible as God's word? Does the Bible say God can't talk to me?"

"I don't think so, but if you believe the Bible is the word of God then you can find your answers there."

"Dad, that's another thing, why should I believe the Bible is the word of God? Just saying it doesn't make it so. But, let's say it is the word of God; then God must have spoken to someone about what to write in it. So then, God should be able to talk to me. Plus reading the Bible is like reading a book written in Greek. I have to rely on others to tell me what it means. I think, people translate the meanings to serve themselves. Different religions accept the parts they like and reject the parts they don't like. Then, they try to convince as many people as possible that their translation is correct. It just doesn't make sense to me. That is why I want to hear from God directly. And one more thing, why is God invisible? Did God appear to Adam and Eve or did the voice come from the sky? I have too many questions and I think people are just making up the answers."

"God wants you to believe in him without needing him to talk to you personally or for you to see him. That is what having faith is all about."

"Why is faith so important to God when all he needs to do is speak up? I don't think making me go to church will make me have faith. I need something more if I'm to believe in something that I can't see, hear or touch."

"You will develop your faith through experience, David. Until then, you will have to rely on my experience and believe that what I tell you is true."

The rest of the ride home is silent, but David's thoughts scare him. He thinks he should have kept his mouth shut. He is worried about the consequences of upsetting his parents if he doesn't agree with them.

A barrage of questions come to him.

Would I suffer now or after I die in that place called hell if I don't have faith? Shouldn't I try to have faith just in case the adults were right? Would my life be better if I just agreed with them? Should I keep any doubts to myself? Should I just tell them what they want to hear so I won't have to deal with their anger or disappointment? Why do mom and dad think controlling what I say and do is important? Why do they want me to be afraid of the same things they fear?

David doesn't like it. When he wants to do something they might disapprove of, he sneaks around and does it behind their backs.

David's mom doesn't go to church much. She stays home taking care of his four-year-old brother, Tommy. Lunch is the big meal on Sunday. She starts preparing it early so the food can be ready by the time David, Michael and dad have returned from church. Other than his dad giving a blessing before eating, God is not mentioned at lunch. Afterward, it is David's job to clear the table. He either washes the dishes or dries them, and then puts them away. Today Michael washes, and David dries.

He spends the rest of the day playing outside without giving another thought to God. He usually looks forward to Sunday nights because that is the only time he is allowed to eat in front of the TV and watch his favorite shows. It is also the only time he is allowed to drink a coke or root beer. Something is different about this night. He hasn't finished the slice of his mom's homemade pizza before he almost falls asleep while his favorite show is still on. With droopy eyes, he heads to his bedroom earlier than usual.

David is already in bed when his mom comes up. "Are you feeling OK, honey?"

"I'm just tired and have a headache."

Mom puts her hand on his forehead. "You're a little warm. You hardly ever have a headache. Maybe you're coming down with something. I'll go get a Tylenol and we'll see how you feel in the morning. In the meantime, say your prayers."

David gets out of bed and kneels down. He recites the prayer he was taught to say but never really understood.

"Now I lay me down to sleep, I pray the Lord my soul to keep, if I should die before I wake, I pray the Lord my soul to take. God bless mom and dad and my brother." Then he adds, "I hope I don't die tonight and I would really like for you to talk to me. I don't even know what the hell my soul is anyway."

By the time mom returns, David is fast asleep. She puts the water and Tylenol on the side table, hugs him and says, "I love you, son." She turns out the lights and tiptoes out the door.

Chapter 2

The Love Game

Monday, June 10

"Wake up David," the strange voice whispers.

"Not now," the eleven-year-old replies, thinking it's mom calling.

"**WAKE UP DAVID**, it's time to play." The mysterious voice is louder now.

David suddenly realizes the voice is neither of his parents'. He bolts up in bed, his heart racing with fear. "What! Who said that?"

"I AM that I AM."

"Who?"

"I AM known by many names throughout history including the name God, by which you know me ... You may also know me as Love. I Am One in the same."

"No, who are you really? I can't see you. Where are you?"

With eyes wide open David tries to locate the source of this stranger's voice inside his room.

"I AM really God, the Divine Love that created the whole universe."

"Oh, sure, and I am a pro baseball player."

"You can't get anything by me, David. You may someday but you're not old enough now."

"Wait, just yesterday in Sunday school, I asked the teacher if God could talk to me directly and I was told in no uncertain terms, no! God only talks to a few select people such as Moses and Jesus. And now here you are, talking to me."

"You were the one that called me in your prayers yesterday."

"I did but I wasn't sure you were real."

"What about now?"

"I'm still not sure. I might be dreaming. Do you talk to anyone who prays to you?"

"Yes, but they don't believe it's me. They ignore my response either because they don't like what I say or they think it is their imagination."

"Okay, God, let's say for a moment that you really are Divine Love. Where is your voice coming from? It sounds a lot like mine?"

"I AM speaking to you through your heart. You are the only one who can hear it. I can make it sound like anyone's voice. Who would you like it to sound like?" After a pause, the voice says, "How about an old man?" A deep raspy voice falls in David's ears.

"I guess the sound of my voice is okay. Where are you anyway? I hope it's not in Heaven. I don't think I'm dead yet, am I?"

"No, David, you are not dead. I AM here and everywhere. You can't see me now but you will later today."

David is still trying to process what is happening when God speaks again.

"I woke you up this morning to ask if you would like to play The Love Game with me today? It will help you get to know me a little better."

Surprised by God's invitation, David's first thought is Why me? "Are you sure you want to play with me? Don't you have wars to stop and people to save?"

"I AM God, I AM sure about everything. You have had doubts about my existence so I am giving you an opportunity to know for yourself the truth about me. So, what do you say, are you ready to play with me?"

"Oh yes! Do you really expect me to refuse God? How do I play The Love Game?" David asks. His heart is now racing with excitement and wonder.

"This is the way to play," the voice that sounds to David like his own continues: "Go to the park and see how many places you can find me. You can't rely on just your eyes. You will also need to listen with an open heart. You don't have to do it alone. You're welcome to ask for help along the way."

"Okay, God. But ... how do I win this game?"

"It is easy David; you win by choosing to play. In fact, the whole world benefits when you play this game."

"I'm not sure I know what you mean when you say 'listen with your heart'," David says.

"Listening to the heart is one of the great challenges that humans face. It means you focus your attention on the present moment not only with your ears but also with your emotions and intuition and inner voice. But here's the catch — it's helpful to ditch your judgmental goggles. You know the ones that separate things into right or wrong, good or bad. The heart only speaks the language of love, none of that fear, hate, or evil stuff. It's like a lovey-dovey radio station, constantly broadcasting messages of kindness and compassion.

"And hey, I might just drop some serious wisdom bombs on you. It might give you a hint about how to serve yourself and others in the moment. But don't expect Me to give you a step-by-step guide or answer all those pesky 'why' questions. Where's the fun in that?

"Remember The Love Game is the perfect opportunity to know me. When listening to another being, look beyond just their words to appreciate their perspectives. When judgmental thoughts do arise, which they will, let them pass on as you refocus on accepting what is in the moment."

"God, I'm still not sure if I'm making this all up. It seems crazy like a dream. I am hearing you right now as something that is coming from inside me that I don't seem to control. I have a wonderful feeling that I can't explain."

"Life IS a dream, my precious one. This wonderful feeling that you are experiencing is a clue to my presence. Okay, David, let's get the party started."

David jumps out of bed, quickly dresses and meets his mom in the kitchen. "Good morning honey, where are you going in such a hurry?" she asks.

"I'm on my way to the park to play a game."

"Well, you should get something to eat before you go."

"I am too excited to eat. I don't want to keep God waiting."

"What do you mean?" his mother says with an amused curl of her mouth.

"God woke me up this morning and asked if I wanted to play The Love Game so that I could get to know God as Love. I was told that if I kept my eyes open and listened with my heart, I would actually see God."

"God talked to you?" his mother says with some hint at surprise. "Are you sure it wasn't just a dream or your imagination?"

"Yes, it is a dream come true. I have been asking God to talk to me and it happened. I am sure it was really God. My heart told me so. Has God ever talked to you, Mom?"

"I've certainly talked to God but God has never said anything back to me and I have no idea what God looks like either. If you want to get to know God better, why not talk to Pastor Smith?"

"Do you think Pastor Smith has seen God?"

"I don't think he has, David."

"Then why would I talk to him instead of talking to God directly? Would the Pastor tell me something that God doesn't know?"

Mom chuckles as she shakes her head. "Mom, I really have to go."

"David, you are not going out of the house without something in your stomach. Now sit down and eat."

David sits with one foot on the floor and the other kneeling on the chair. His mother turns for a moment, and that's all the time David needs to wolf down his breakfast.

Impatient to start the Game, David jumps up and runs for the door. "Bye, mom, I'll tell you about God when I get back home." A moment later, David is already running down the street and he doesn't hear his mother wishing him good luck.

Dad enters the kitchen. "Who were you wishing good luck?"

"It was David. He is on his way to the park to see God."

Dad looks out the window and sees David. "Is he skipping up the road?"

Mom takes a peek and says, "It looks more like he's dancing." She then relates what David told her about the Game he was playing.

"That kid has such a wild imagination," Dad says.

"But what if in my wildest imagination, David really did hear God talk to him?"

Dad just shakes his head. "Don't be silly."

With one eyebrow raised and head tilted, she responds, "Just saying."

At the park, David says, "Okay, God, what now?"

Chapter 3

In the Clouds

"I AM here David and I appreciate your enthusiasm."

"I'm not sure what to do, God," David says.

"Start where you are David. What is the first thing that catches your eye?"

David looks up through the crack in the trees, thinking that's where God probably hangs out. He notices a beautiful cloud in the sky. "Ok, I see a cloud. What next?"

"Have a chat with the cloud, get to know it and then decide for yourself whether you see me or not. I am offering a clue to start you off. You are more likely to see me in what you are grateful for."

"Hi, white fluffy one," David says, squinting at the cloud. "Thank you for being here. It's the rain you bring that makes the plants grow and fills the rivers and lakes. I love how you provide shade on hot and sunny days. I enjoy how your shape keeps changing as you float across the sky. Sometimes

I see your shape as a face or animal. I imagine flying through you like a bird."

David pauses and wonders how he should go on. Then he says, "I wonder what it is like viewing life from up there. I especially like how you and the sun work together to create beautiful rainbows. Oh, fluffy one, please tell me more about yourself. I would like to get to know you better."

"Hi David, I am Cloud at this moment. Thank you for appreciating me. I am actually one form of water and I've got many names depending on what I look like at the moment. Without me, there would be no life as you know it on earth. I am constantly changing my form. You may also see me as rain, snow, ice, or see me flowing down a river, as crashing waves on the beach or reflecting a sunset on a quiet lake. Sometimes I am dark and other times I let the light through. I can also be invisible when I am humidity. It was I who surrounded you when you've been in the fog. I can be gentle enough to wash a newborn baby or be powerful enough to create the Grand Canyon. You may also enjoy me as you sled down a snowy slope, or dive into the home of water beings. Do you know that I am also inside you? Most of your body is water. I AM in every cell of your body. Do you remember seeing me come out of your mouth on a cold morning? I am there every time you breathe. You just can't see me until the conditions are right. We are never apart. So, David, what brings you out to the park on this glorious day?"

"I am so grateful for your presence and all you do. I am amazed to know that we are a part of each other. I am playing The Love Game with God today. The game is to discover God in as many places as I can find. I want to see God but I don't know what God looks like. Do you have any suggestions?"

"I have not seen God but I have felt God's presence," the cloud says. "The Divine Spirit that is called God is what moves me across the sky, and changes my shape and form and connects me to life. When you feel connected to another being, God is there. I have seen the way you and Tree sway together as one from the same force that moves me. Tree over there has been watching us talk. Maybe the connection you and her have will reveal God to you."

22

"Bye cloud, thanks for your help," David says as he sees the cloud beginning to float across the sky.

"Do you see Me, David?" God asks. "I AM here."

David says, "No God, all I saw was Cloud but I'll keep looking." He runs over to the tree and gives it a big hug. He climbs midway up before finding a nice branch to sit on.

Chapter 4

Up a Tree

"Hi Tree. Remember me?"

"Yes, I do. If it isn't my favorite tree-climbing buddy, David?"

"I want you to know how much I love climbing up onto your high branches. I can see so much farther. You have been a safe place for me to go when I have been upset. When we sway together in the wind, I hold you tight and feel really connected to you as if we were one being."

A soft rustle skirted the boughs drooping around David before the tree said, "I too enjoy our connection. I mean, who wouldn't love being hugged by a human like you David? I am energized by your embraces, and I'm always happy to be here for you when you are upset."

"I want to know more about you, Tree, " David said. "I am the one who usually does most of the talking when I sit in your arms. I am ready to listen to you now."

"David, I know I am a part of nature and nature is God. God connects me to the earth with deep roots, and connects me to the sky with my branches. It connects me to the sun as I absorb the warmth. When the wind touches me, my leaves sing and my limbs dance with joy. The rain's life force nurtures my growth. God has many purposes for me being here. I am a home to birds and squirrels. I am a sanctuary for young ones like yourself, holding you in my arms when you are lonely or sad and listening to your stories. I offer shade and protection to the newborn plants growing around me. My fruits, nuts and sap nurture many different beings. I clean the air you breathe. What I breathe out is what you breathe in. I can be transformed into building materials for art, furniture and houses. For many people, I am the fuel for their fires that warm them and cook their food. I don't have any resistance to God's purpose, I am what I am."

"Wow Tree. I have always known how valuable your presence has been for me. Knowing how you serve all of life on earth amazes me. I want to be appreciated and valued like you, so, I, too, can be of service to others someday."

"Not someday, David," Tree says. "The same God that has given me purpose has given you a valuable purpose for every second of your life. Since we are all connected, your purpose will also serve all. So, David, what has led you to me today?"

"I am playing a game with God. The game is about finding God in as many places as I can. If I listen with my heart and keep my eyes open God would be revealed to me. God said I could ask for help. What do you say my friend, can you help me find God?"

Tree says, "The message that is coming through me is about compassion. Compassion is what you experience when you feel connected to another being who is suffering and you want to help ease their pain."

"It's something like you being there for me when I need it," David says.

"I suppose so. There is a little girl over there sitting on a park bench crying. Compassion opens your heart and eyes to God's presence."

"Thank you, Tree, for allowing me to get to know you and also for your help. Bye now. See you later."

26

"Do you see Me, David?" God asks. "I AM here."

"I hear you and feel your presence but I only see the Tree. I'm not going to give up trying." He climbs down the tree and heads over to the little girl sitting on the bench.

Chapter 5

Compassionate Hearts

David stands looking at the girl for some moments. She does not sense his approach until he says, "Hi, I am David. Is it ok if I sit with you?"

The little girl looks up and wipes her tears away. She doesn't reply for several seconds and simply gazes at the boy standing close to the bench. Then she says, "I am Angela and, yes, I would be nice to have you sit with me."

"I notice you are crying Angela. Anything that I could help with?"

"I am sad that no one wants to play with me."

David offers her a smile. "I don't know exactly what you are going through but I am an expert on loneliness. I spend most of my days by myself and it hurts when I see other kids having fun playing together. Is there anything I can do?"

"Thanks for offering, David. Maybe you can just sit and be with me for a while."

David and Angela sit in silence as they think about each other's loneliness. David is surprised when tears well up in his eyes too. After a while, appreciation for each other's presence emerges. The sadness lifts and then simultaneously David and Angela look into each other's eyes. The tears turn to smiles and then to giggles.

"Thanks for being here. I feel so much better," Angela says.

"You're welcome, but I really didn't do anything."

"You didn't have to do anything, David. You showed up. I am glad you didn't tell me that I shouldn't feel sad. A lot of times when I have been feeling bad or angry, my Nana tells me I should look on the bright side and appreciate what I have because things could be much worse. But her advice has the opposite effect on me because I feel worse when I can't switch away from my negative thoughts. What I really want is to be accepted and to be held. I know she means well but I don't want to be treated like I am broken and need to be fixed."

Angela suddenly falls quiet after she had spoken. David had listened intently and realizes how much he can relate to the feelings of this girl he is meeting for the first time. He feels an unfamiliar closeness to her. He reaches over and holds her hand. "I know we just met, Angela, but I feel I have known you for a long time."

Angela says, "Me too."

David says, "How come I haven't seen you before?"

"I moved here two months ago with my brother and mother to live with my Nana. You are the first person I've met outside the hospital."

"Hospital? Are you sick?"

"Yes, I'm getting treatment for cancer."

David's eyebrows arch a little. "That must be scary. I notice you are wearing a hat and it's the middle of the summer. Are you cold?"

"No, I don't have any hair."

"How come? Did someone cut it off?"

"The drugs they gave me made most of my hair fall out. It looked stupid to have only a few hairs so I cut them off."

"Oh, I am so sorry. How are you feeling now?"

"I'm tired most of the time. It may be the side effects of the drugs. I don't think I'm getting any better."

30

After some thought, David says, "You didn't mention your Dad. Did he come to live with your Nana too?"

"My mother wasn't sure who my father was. She was friends with many men. My Momma did a pretty good job of being a single mother until I got sick. That's when she became depressed, started drinking alcohol a lot and I think she got into other drugs too. One time she left my brother and me alone for a long time and I got scared that something bad happened to her. I called 911 and the next thing I knew a social worker was threatening to take us away from her. My Nana stepped in and told them she would take care of us until Momma got better. Soon after we moved to live with Nana, Momma left us. Nana told me she was in a hospital across town. She almost died of an overdose of alcohol and drugs. I hope she gets better soon. I miss her."

"I think I should say something but I can't find the words, Angela."

"That's okay, you don't have to say anything. Let's lighten the mood. When, I get better, I am going to be in the fifth grade. How about you, David?"

"I'm going to be in the fifth grade too. Maybe we will be in the same class. Isn't this a great day to meet each other? I think we are going to be good friends."

"Enough about me," Angela says. Did you come to the park to play today?"

"Yes. Today I am playing a game with God." David relates the story about talking to God and The Love Game God invited him to play. "I hope to really see God today. I was sitting up in the tree over there and Tree suggested I might find God being here with you."

Angela's eyes widen as she holds a curled finger against her lip. "Oh my God, you're the boy in the tree."

"What are you talking about Angela?" David says.

"Two days ago, I drew a picture of a boy sitting in a tree. I don't know why the image came to me. He looked sad that day. I'll show you." Angela opened her drawing pad and found the picture. "See?"

Surprise presses over David's face. "Angela, I was sitting in a tree two days ago in the woods behind my house. I was talking to God and I was sad and angry that He wasn't talking back to me." After a pause, he says, "By the way, you are a very good artist."

"Thank you. I drew another picture of the boy the same day." Angela flips through her drawing pad to stop at the picture of the boy petting a deer.

"How could you know that when I climbed down the tree a deer came up to me and she allowed me to pet her?"

"I don't know," she says. "Those images just came to me. I had hoped to meet that boy someday. Then today, you came and sat beside me. This is really strange." She falls into silence again. Then she speaks. "I have been praying for God to take this cancer away so my Momma can come home. I don't know if I really believe in God. Nana says I need to have faith and continue to pray. I can't see that my prayers have helped. I've asked God why he allowed me to get sick but I haven't got any answers yet. Did God really talk to you? You mean He really exists? I don't know anyone that God has spoken to, nor do I know anyone who has seen God."

"I hear the same thing about faith," David says. "I was very skeptical if there even was such a thing as God. I asked him to talk to me or appear to me so I could know for sure. No matter how many times I pleaded for him to talk to me, he never responded. At least that was so up until this morning when He woke me up."

David pauses for a moment to gauge Angela's response. She leans forward on the bench, her eyes wide with wonder, fixed on David's face with an intensity that makes him catch his breath. The usual wall of wariness that illness had built around her seems to crumble as hope and curiosity light up her features. She unconsciously holds her breath, waiting for him to continue, as if his next words might unlock a door she hadn't known existed.

David continues, "God tells me to listen with my heart and keep my eyes open and I would get to know what God looks like."

"Angela, it's time to go," her grandma calls out, jarring them both from their shared enchantment.

"Okay," Angela yells back. "That's my Nana there with my younger brother, Sammy, on the swings. I would love to play the Love Game with you and God but I have to go home now.

32

I feel so much better David. Your compassion is just what I needed. See that old woman struggling to carry her groceries over there? I bet she could use some of your kindness. I think God likes kind acts."

"Thanks for your suggestion," David says. "Can we meet tomorrow here and I'll show you around the park. There are many fun things to do here together. I'll let you know if I see God."

"I AM here. Do you see me now?" a voice sounds in David's heart.

"I hear you God, but I only see Angela. You must still be invisible."

Angela takes a look around the area surrounding the bench before saying, "Were you just talking to God, David? What did he say?"

"God said, I AM here. Do you see me now?"

"David, I want you to know that it is very important for me to see you again. I will be here tomorrow. Can you give me a hug before I leave?"

"Sure." David and Angela's hug is brief but heartfelt before they head off their separate ways.

On the walk home, Angela, Nana and Sammy hear loud yelling coming from the back of a house they are passing. They keep walking when they see a boy about Angela's age being berated by a man that Angela assumes is his father. She hears the father say, "Can't you do anything right, you moron?" before he slaps the kid in the back of the head. Witnessing the sudden violence makes Angela's stomach clench as tremors of fear and anxiety course through her body.

Sammy says, "That sounds really scary to me. Let's get out of here."

They pick up speed to get away as fast as possible. Even after they are home, Angela can't shake off her concern for the boy. "Nana, I hope he will be alright."

"So do I," Nana says.

Chapter 6

Open-Hearted Kindness

The elderly woman is stooped over a cane in her right hand and a big bag of groceries in her left. She looks nervously at the young boy who comes running toward her. David hesitates for a moment to catch his breath. "Hi, I am David, can I carry your bag for you?"

"Why would you want to do that for me?"

"I noticed you are stopping frequently and might be out of breath. I thought I would be friendly and offer to help."

"I don't have any money, young man."

"Oh, I don't want any money," he says as he reaches for her grocery bag. "I'm David. What's your name?"

"Well, okay, I am Mrs. Deera," she says, her shoulders relaxing visibly as she hands over the heavy bag.

They continue walking together. Mrs. Deera asks David, "Don't you have something better to do than helping an old lady? Maybe playing in the park?"

"Actually Mrs. Deera, I am playing. I am playing a game with God today." He tells her how he was awakened by a strange voice that morning and about his conversation with God. "My friend told me that God may show up in the presence of kindness and suggested I might offer some kindness to you. So here I am."

"That is the craziest thing I have ever heard in my eighty years," the old woman says. "God is a spirit. You can't see a spirit." Mrs. Deera continues saying, "And spirits don't talk either. It's all just your imagination and a waste of your time."

"I thought you might have known God, Mrs. Deera, because you have lived a long life and have experienced many things."

"Yes, I have lived a long life, David, and I have suffered much. I think God has abandoned me because my prayers to ease my suffering haven't been answered. I have lost my husband, daughter and many friends. Now I am lonely and I'm not in the best of health. I don't know why God doesn't just take me and ease my suffering."

Suddenly David hears the voice. "David, I want you to give a message to Mrs. Deera for me since she has not yet opened her heart to my presence."

David turns to the lady and says, "Oh, my Gosh, Mrs. Deera. God led me to you today so I could give you this message. I am to tell you that God is with you now and has always been here for you throughout your suffering. God was with you when your husband Robert died last year after a stroke and then your best friend Mary died two months ago after suffering from breast cancer. He was with you even when Maggie passed.

Mrs. Deera is thunderstruck.

David adds, "I am with you now through the pain in your back. You are not alone. Your suffering has been accompanied by many gifts which you will discover as you open your heart to the Love that is within you. Even your physical limitations are giving you an opportunity to direct your attention to me as Love. The value of your presence alone is fulfilling my purpose for your creation. You have much to give the world by just being Amma. And, today you are an important part of the game I am playing with David."

Amma's eyebrows lift in surprise. "What the hell, David? How did you know my first name and the names of my husband Robert, and best friend Mary and how they died? How could you know that I was suffering with pain in my back? Have we met before? Who told you these things?"

"No, Mrs. Deera, we haven't met before. I am just as surprised as you. I didn't know your husband's or friend's name or that you had back pain before the words came out of my mouth. But God knows all about you."

Mrs. Deera is completely lost for words.

How is this possible, she thinks?

David and Mrs. Deera continue walking silently, dumbfounded by their experience, until they reach her door. He takes her groceries inside, puts them on the kitchen table then stops to look deeply into her eyes. Her eyes start to water like his. She thanks him with a hug. No more words need to be spoken. Both of them realize something special has happened as a warm, comforting feeling flows through their bodies.

Mrs. Deera wipes her eyes and says, "Would you like to sit and have some milk and cookies with me for a few minutes?"

"Sure, that sounds great." David sits down at the table and notices the photos on the dining room cabinet. He gets up to take a closer look. One picture shows Amma and Robert.

Amma tells him, "That picture was taken on our 55th wedding anniversary. The picture next to it is of my son and his family. My son, Mark, is a doctor at the hospital. Next to him is his daughter, Sara, who is in college. She doesn't know what she wants to do yet but I think she is leaning toward becoming a doctor like her dad. And his wife, Ellen. She is an artist. Mark and Ellen are now divorced. I think his long hours at the hospital took its toll. But I keep the picture of them together as a reminder of the good times."

David points to another picture with a boy who looks his age standing next to an older girl in it. "Who's in this picture?"

"That's Mark when he was about your age and his sister, Maggie, who was 13 at the time. She suffered from depression. We couldn't understand how such a young person could suffer from depression. We took her to a doctor who counseled her and treated her with different medications." With tears in her eyes and a crackling in her voice, she continues. "When Maggie was 15, we came home and found her dead with her wrist cut. I'm sorry, David, you don't need to know that."

David says, "thanks for telling me. I'm okay. Please continue."

For a long time, Robert and I blamed ourselves, blamed the doctors, and blamed the school system. But mostly, we blamed God. How could he let this happen? It was a really stressful time for our marriage. I can't believe I'm telling you all of this. How old are you anyway?"

"I'm eleven."

"Well, I've never been so relaxed around an eleven-year-old.   She continues to say, "Mark shut down, wouldn't talk. We were really hesitant at first to trust any doctor or counselor but Mark was so distressed that we had to. We were pleased to see that the counseling visits really helped him through his grief. I think his experience with his sister's death was a motivating factor for him becoming a psychiatrist. He wanted to help people before they became desperate to the point of taking their own life. Just talking about Maggie still brings up some deep sadness for me."

"You said you were lonely," David says. "Doesn't your family keep you company?"

"I really miss Sara. She used to come by frequently but now she is away at school. Mark comes by occasionally for lunch and some holidays but he is so busy, he doesn't find the time for much more than quick visits. Ellen and I have never been close so I only see her on special occasions. She is a caregiver for her father who is ill. Here are your cookies and milk."

"These chocolate chip cookies are my favorite and they taste yummy, Mrs. Deera."

"I'm glad you like them. I don't know why I baked them today. I don't eat them myself. Cookies aren't on my diabetic diet but something told me that I might have a visitor today."

"I sure am glad you baked them, they hit the spot. Thank you. I want to continue playing the Love Game, Mrs. Deera, can you give me any clues to where I might see God?"

"I don't know about seeing God but I have felt God was present when I was feeling Love. Like right now. I love the time we spent together today, David. I just realized it is the first time in a while that I haven't been focused on my pain. I can't thank you enough. Maybe letting Love be your guide will take you to God. Before you leave David, I want to give you a gift for your quest."

Mrs. Deera fetches a small bag from another room and puts it on the kitchen table. "This contains something for the Love you will find today. But wait until you get back to the park to open it. You will know the right time. I have a feeling it is going to be helpful."

"Thanks for the gift, it was nice meeting you, Mrs. Deera. Bye."

The voice reaches David again. "I AM here David. Can you see me now?"

"I can only see Mrs. Deera," David says. "I was listening with my heart and related your message to her. I have my eyes wide open but I couldn't see you. Am I getting closer to seeing you?"

"You are much closer than you think David. I continue to be invisible to you because you have more things to learn. Mrs. Deera's suggestion to let Love be your guide is a great clue."

As David walks back to the park he repeats, "I will see God where I find Love, I will see God where I find Love."

Chapter 7

Nature Wisdom

David sits down on a bench under a tree. He can still taste the chocolate chip cookies. His mom would bake chocolate chip cookies on special occasions, and he always felt warmth and appreciation when he ate them. He placed the small brown bag on the bench.

He says to himself, "okay, David, where can I find Love?" He has only heard his Mom say the word, and he learned to say it back to her. He was told in Sunday school that Jesus loves him because the Bible says so. But no one actually said what that means. And how could a dead person love someone they don't even know? He thought love might mean that you were liked more than a lot. He knew he felt safe and comforted when his mother hugged him and told him how much she loved him. Did she still love him when she spanked him or punished him? When she punished him, his security vanished in a storm of fear. The pain of rejection was worse than the physical pain. She could whip Love away if he did anything wrong. Does God judge like his mother, or is Divine Love different from human love? Does he really send people he loves to hell if they disobey him? Is that Divine Love?

The sound of "chicka-dee-dee-dee, chicka-dee-dee-dee." interrupted David's parade of thoughts and questions. "Chicka-dee-dee-dee." Suddenly, a beautiful little bird flies down onto the arm of the bench next to where he put the bag Mrs. Deera had given him.

"Hi, little bird, I am David. I really like your singing and what a nice surprise it is that you are coming to sit with me.

"Hi David, I AM Chickadee. I AM curious about what is in the bag."

David had forgotten to look in the bag. "Well, Chickadee, Mrs. Deera gave me this to give to the Love that I will find. I think this may be a good time to check it out."

He opens the top that had been neatly folded over to find bird seed. He wonders how she knew he would meet Chickadee and how he loved birds. Maybe she had finally opened her heart to God. He reaches into the bag, puts a few seeds in his palm, and extends it to Chickadee. The tiny bird jumps right on the end of his fingers. She was so light in David's hand. They look into each other's eyes just like he did with Angela and Mrs. Deera. A feeling of a deep connection emerges in his heart. He had never been so close to a wild bird before. This feeling reminded him of what he experienced two days ago when he looked into the eyes of the deer. Chickadee inspects the seeds and carefully chooses one before flying up into the tree. A few minutes later, she returns for another morsel. She repeats this several times. Then she just sits looking at David.

"Are you storing the seeds in your nest," David asks.

"No," said Chickadee. "I have chicks."

"Wow! I love that I can offer something to help nurture your babies. I feel blessed that you trust me not to hurt you. Aren't you afraid of me?"

"I am not afraid because you have radiant Love shining from your heart."

Chickadee said, "Plus, I don't need to trust you. I trust myself and my inner Nature to know what will serve me and what will not. I live in the moment since I have no imagination to create fear. I keep my eyes open and if I see a hawk that may want to hurt me, I just fly into a dense bush until it passes. I don't have to tell my chicks to be afraid to sit on a branch because it might break. Instead, I show them how to fly so they can live in joy."

"Thank you so much for your wise perspective, Chickadee. I am playing a game with God today. God asks me to discover all the places I might see God. God also tells me to let Love be my guide. That seems to be what you do to care for yourself and your chicks. You have an inner knowing that I would not hurt you. I wonder if that is instinct, intuition, or God speaking to you?"

"Maybe it's all three, divinely connected, David."

"I am so grateful that God has led me to you today, Chickadee. I know God must be close because of how I feel spending this time with you. Can you offer any more clues to where I might find God?"

"You said it, David. The feeling that you have lets you know that God is close. Since God is always present, and this special feeling you have is not, then maybe your thoughts are keeping you feeling apart from God instead of a part of God. Remember you are playing the Love Game. Consider replacing the word 'God' with 'Love' and explore how viewing the present moment from that perspective will help you see what you are looking for."

"Thanks, I will take your suggestion."

"I have one more invitation, David, that might help. I love my wildness, and I feel free and full of joy when I'm flying. Love is with me. Maybe you will see Love when you feel free and full of joy. Be a little wild and wander off the beaten path."

"Thanks again for your presence, Chickadee, and for seeing the Love radiating from my heart. I'm going to pour the seeds out on the bench here for you and others who might appreciate something to eat."

"Hey David, I AM here. Can you see me now?"

"No, God. I loved my experience with Chickadee and knew you were here, but I could only see Chickadee. Am I playing the Game wrong?"

"David, you are playing the game perfectly. You are learning a lot through this game, and each step you take will be perfect and will lead you to know and see me."

"Alright then, I'll keep at it. Oh, by the way, Chickadee suggested that maybe it would help me see you if I refer to you as Love. Is that OK?"

"We are one and the same, David."

"Ok, Love. What direction do I head in to find joy?" David closed his eyes and spun in a circle. He stopped after a few turns and started walking in the direction he was facing, not knowing what joy he would find.

Chapter 8

Joyful Guidance

David notices how alive his senses have become. He sees beauty everywhere. He takes his shoes off and walks on the soft grass. He stops and smells the flowers and hears the honeybees gathering nectar. The warmth of the sun bathes his body. He stops to take a sip from the water fountain and appreciates the coolness. He continues to walk alongside a paved winding path. He hears kids playing and wonders if that is the direction that will lead to joy. Out of the corner of his eyes David sees a rabbit on the edge of the woods.

The rabbit calls to David's heart "come this way."

David goes over to the calmly sitting, "hi Rabbit, you called me?"

"Hello David, yes, I called you. I wanted to let you know that you might find your joy wandering away from the paved path."

"Wait", replies David, "how did you know my name?"

"Love told me you were coming."

"Are you going to guide me into the woods?" David asks.

"No, your Joy will be discovering the treasures found while exploring the mystery of uncertainty. You will create your own path. Like I AM, the treasures you will find are the guides that show up on your journey. Remember, joy is in the moment, not the past and not the future. Have fun".

"Thank you, Rabbit, I really appreciate your help." The Rabbit scampers off on his own adventure.

David takes a moment to put his shoes back on before he heads into the woods. He carefully avoids stepping on any plants. He pushes away low-lying sapling branches and snakes his way around some bushes. He hears water flowing and shifts his direction to the sound. He follows a narrow trail that animals have created until he reaches the edge of a small stream. He looks at the glistening stones, half in the water and half out. The light reflecting off the ripples mesmerizes him. David has always enjoyed finding colorful rocks with interesting patterns. He picks up a couple of the rocks for a close-up view and then returns them. He walks over to one big rock that drew his attention. He hears the rock say, "turn me over, David." He rolls the rock over to find a lovely quartz crystal resting in the depression left by the rock.

"Oh, my God, I mean Love," David blurts out with elation. He picks the crystal up and gently brushes off the sand that was sticking on its surface. He finds a comfortable spot to sit on the edge of the stream and holds it up allowing the light to shine.

"Hey beautiful gem, my name is David. How is it that you have come into my life now?"

"I AM Crystal. I have been waiting for you to find me. I AM here to show you how the two of us are alike."

"What do you mean Crystal?"

"Tell me David, what do you experience when you look at me?"

David is filled with joy as he inspects all facets of the treasure. "Crystal, I see smooth surfaces, rough surfaces, very clear areas and some cloudy spaces. I see light hitting cracks in your inside that are splitting into sparkling rainbow colors. You are unique and beautiful. I sense that you hold a wisdom within you that you have longed to share.

46

I think you might be a healer. I feel warm inside and I can't stop smiling. I AM immensely grateful for this opportunity to be with you."

"What you describe is yourself David."

David's eyes tear. "Wow," says David, "I have never thought of myself that way. Yet, my tears screamed 'yes' when you said I was describing myself."

Crystal explains, "My gift is my ability to reflect the wisdom found in the Love that you are. I can clarify the answers to many of the questions you have."

"I AM here."

David realizes that he had been so immersed in the moment that he had forgotten about playing the game with Love. "Oh, Crystal I have been playing a game with Love. You know, God. I'm trying to see how many places I could find and see him. I know Love is here but I have not been able to see him yet. Do you have any suggestions?"

Crystal says to David, "Expectations of what Love/God should or shouldn't look like will blind you. Let go of judgments, open your eyes and allow your heart to show you a new way of seeing the world. The peaceful pond at the end of this stream is a perfect place to reflect on and release the judgments that keep you from seeing Love."

"Crystal, would you like to come home with me? I would really enjoy caring for you."

Crystal says, "absolutely." David smiles, holds Crystal to his heart and says, "we are going to have so much fun playing The Love Game."

Together they follow the stream to the pond.

Chapter 9

Peace Pond

The gurgling stream sounds fade as it pours into the silence of the pond. David is amazed at how still and mirror-like the pond is. David takes Crystal from his pocket, and together, they sit on the soft bank at the edge of the pond. He takes his shoes off and lets his feet dangle into the water.

David asks Crystal, "What now?"

"Would you like to get to know more about the gifts of this peaceful pond?" Crystal asks.

"That's a great idea." "Hi, Pond, I am David, and I am here with Crystal. I appreciate your calmness and silence. Sitting here, I feel a deep sense of peace as if everything is perfect at this moment."

"Hello, David and Crystal, I AM the Peace Pond. Thank you for visiting me. I AM the home that the twisting and burbling stream flows into. You feel the perfection of this moment because that is my nature. I know that you came to see Love or God. You are in the right place. Look at me and tell me what you see."

David says, "I see a few water bugs dancing on the surface, and there are reflections of the clouds and the tree leaves. There is a bird flying overhead, and I see its reflection move across the water."

"That's fine, David, now look deeper."

"I can see a few minnows darting around, and a few are coming up to kiss my toes. The bottom is sandy with a few small rocks."

"Do you see anything else, David?"

"Oh," David says, "there is a reflection of myself sitting at your edge."

Love says, "I AM Here."

"Come on, Love, I don't see you."

"Are your eyes open, David?"

"You know they are. This game is really hard."

"Your eyes might be open, but you are trying to see me through the darkness of judgments and expectations. Let the Peace Pond help you release those judgments, and you will see Me in the light."

"What do you think God should look like?" asks Pond.

"Doesn't the Bible say God created us in his own image?" asks David.

"Yes, that is a perspective that many people believe and many people don't. There are many interpretations of that passage. If humans look like God physically, it would be hard to know what God really looks like since people's appearances are all unique.

"We always refer to him as Father in heaven, so he must be a man. I have seen pictures of Jesus. Maybe God looks like an old Jesus."

"David, maybe the reason that you have not seen God today yet is because you are expecting a man to appear. As Crystal told you, your expectations have blinded you, even though you have been told many times, 'I AM here.' These expectations have come from what you have been told based on beliefs that have been passed down through hundreds of generations. Different cultures have different beliefs. I'm going to suggest that we do a little ceremony to release your judgments and your beliefs about what you have been told about God and let the Truth reveal itself to you personally. Is that okay?"

David nods.

"Pick up a pebble that will represent something you think you know about God and throw it into me. I can handle it."

"God is a man." David throws the pebble into the pond. There is a brief splash, a few ripples spread out, and the pond quickly returns to its peace.

"God is separate from me, and lives in heaven."

David throws another pebble in. With each thought, He continues to throw pebbles into the Peace Pond.

"I will only see God after I die and only if I have been good and follow the rules." And he rattled off all the ideas adults have stuffed his head with.

"God only looks like a human."

"God looks like an old Jesus, and he wears a long white robe."

"God will judge me and decide if I will go to heaven or hell."

"God will only appear when he needs to do something great, and then only to religious people."

"God has a halo over his head and is always surrounded by angels."

"God is invisible because he is only spirit."

"Maybe he looks like a ghost that can walk through walls."

"God always looks the same."

"Do you have any more expectations?" Pond of Peace asks.

"Probably, but I can't think of any right now." David replies.

Pond asks David, "When you asked God this morning who was calling your name to wake you up, what was God's reply?"

"I AM What I Am. I AM known by many names. God is one you know me as. You may also know me as Love," David replies.

"Maybe it will be more helpful now to take Chickadee's suggestion and shift your perspective and consider what Love looks like rather than what God looks like? Now,

David, with an open mind and heart, how would you recognize Divine Love if you gazed upon it? I'll let you and Crystal sit with that question.

  While you do, I invite you to close your eyes for a few moments and notice your breath, David. Allow any thoughts that come to flow out with your breath. They will merge with me just like the stream does and the pebbles that you tossed into my depth did."

  David's eyes close, and his thoughts come and go as they flow into the pond: Isn't Love just a feeling? What does Divine Love look like? Maybe it looks like a perfect combination of gratitude, connection, compassion, kindness, love, joy, and peace. Perhaps I will never see Love. What is Love anyway? Can words define it? I just don't know.

  "What do you think, Crystal? Why isn't Crystal saying anything? Maybe I won't see God or Love after all. Should I go home? The thoughts and words space out. He continues to notice his breath, and the one word arises that he finds himself repeating, "Perfect - Perfect - Perfect."

  Suddenly, David opens his eyes and bursts out with excitement. "OH MY GOD, I see you. I get it. Love is the Peace Pond."

  Love says, "YES! And......"

52

Chapter 10

Seen As Love

"What are you getting at Love? Is there more?"

"Where else have you seen me today? How many times have I told you that "I AM here?""

"A bunch of times," David recalled.

What were you focused on when you heard me say, "I AM here."

David said, "When I first started playing the Game, I was looking at Cloud with gratitude. Do you mean that you are Cloud?"

"I sure do," said Love.

David continued," Then there was Tree. I felt a close connection with. Of course, I saw you as Tree. I experienced compassion with Angela and had that wonderful feeling when I looked into her eyes; I had feelings of appreciation, connection, and joy. I saw you as Angela. Oh yes, that happened again when I looked into the kind eyes of Mrs. Deera and the loving eyes of Chickadee while she sat in my hand. I saw both of them as you Love. appreciation, connection, compassion, kindness, love, and joy were all present. There you were as Rabbit who guided me to joy. Then I met you as Crystal. I was feeling such joy realizing how you brought us together, and together we journeyed to the Pond of Peace, where I was finally able to let go of my expectations and beliefs and see you."

"There was something you forgot to mention," Love said. "You saw me in one other place that you passed over."

David reran the events of the day and couldn't recall anything else he had seen where Love told him, "I AM here."

Crystal reminded him, "You heard I AM here when you were looking into the Pond.

David thought back and remembered he saw a few reflections. But he didn't connect the reflections with God.

Crystal reminded him, "David, one of the reflections you saw was yourself. You saw your Loveself reflected in the Pond of Peace."

"Oh no, not me!" David incredulously responds, "You don't mean that I was seeing Love as me."

Crystal says, "Of course, David, you are here. Because of your experiences with rejection, abandonment, punishment, and fear, I know it may be hard for you to see yourself in a non-judgmental, accepting way that reflects Divine Love. Humans have created the illusion that they are separate from each other as well as from God. In Truth, there is no separation. Everything that exists in form and in spirit is part of the Oneness of Divine Love, including you. We are one body created by the mystery of divine love, and every part has a purpose." "Okay, David, say it," Crystal urges.

With a little hesitation, David says, "I AM part of the one body that is called God. I AM here as Divine Love."

Crystal adds, "The only thing that can separate you from God and the Truth of who you are... are your thoughts. And David, one of the gifts God has given to you as a form of itself is the freedom to choose your thoughts and actions. It is your choice to see yourself as one with Divine Love or not."

"Now David, my child, you have heard, seen me, and have learned a little more about the Truth of the Oneness of

Divine Love. The Love Game that you have been playing is not about searching for me because I am always here. I AM always here as your Perfect Love-Self. When you choose to let go of judgments and be the Love that you are, you will radiate this image to the universe. You then will see me reflected in everything your eyes and heart focus on. You also know that I may speak to you in any form, such as Cloud, Tree, Chickadee, Crystal, Pond of Peace, or another person. I can also speak to you without a form such as angels or souls of myself, including your own soul. You will know the message is from me only when it nurtures the Oneness of Love."

David heads back home and comments to Crystal that he feels wonderful in a way he has never experienced before.

"Can you describe this feeling, David?"

After a few moments of silence, David says, "I can't seem to find the right words. I think it might be a combination of many positive feelings all mixed together. I feel calm yet full of energy. I feel joyful excitement. I also feel an intense level of appreciation for this moment. I feel as if I am floating in the sky, looking down at a beautiful movie of us walking home together with all the beings around us smiling. There is a peaceful feeling that all is perfect. I love this moment, and I don't want it to end. That's it, Crystal. I am feeling Perfect."

Crystal asks David, "Would you agree that the Perfect feeling you have is Divine Love?" David just smiled the rest of the way home.

Chapter 11

Dad's Fear

David's mother hurried to greet him when she heard the door open. There was a big smile on his face when he entered.

"Hi, honey, how was your day? You must be hungry. Did you see God?"

David replied, "I had a perfect day. Yes, I am very hungry, and yes, I did see God today."

"You actually saw God?"

"Yes, Mom, I saw God lots of times today and in many places. Instead of using the name God, I am now referring to God as Love. You know they are one and the same."

"Wow! Dinner is almost ready. Sit down and tell me about your day."

"I went to the park as Love asked me to. Once there, I asked for Love's help to start the game. Love told me to allow my attention to focus on something; it doesn't matter what it is. It could be anything: an object, animal, or person.

Express my appreciation for its presence and have a conversation with it so that I can learn more about it. He reminded me to listen with my heart and keep my eyes open. I started with Cloud, then Tree, Angela, Mrs. Deera, Chickadee, Rabbit, Crystal, and finally Peace Pond."

"So, David, what does God or Love look like?"

"Love looks like you, mom, or me, or whatever you look at when your heart is open and your mind has let go of judgments. But you will recognize God only if you are experiencing Love because God is Love. Also, you might not see Love if you have expectations or beliefs about what it should be or look like. My expectations got me hung up for a while until I could let them go into the Peace Pond. I knew Love was around because I could hear Love's voice tell me, 'I AM here,' but I couldn't see Love for a long time. Then, all at once, there it was, right before my eyes. Crystal helped me realize that I had been seeing Love all day. 'Love is everywhere. Whatever I am focusing on is a reflection of Divine Love if I choose to see it that way.' I learned that there is nothing but Love, and everything we see is a part of that Oneness. It would be impossible for Love not to be present. That would be like me going out of the house and leaving my heart in my bedroom. It is people who have created separation and judgments that blind us to the presence of Love. Other animals and beings in nature told me they are not separate from Love because Love is their Nature. Love has given humans a special gift, and that gift is choice. The choice is to play the Love Game and see the world through Love's eyes or stay separate from Love."

David's mother is astonished that David could possibly know these things. It certainly wasn't anything she or his dad taught him. She asked, "Really, who told you these things?"

"I told you, Mom, it was Love. But sometimes Love spoke as Cloud, Tree, Angela, Mrs. Deera, Chickadee, Rabbit, Crystal, and the Pond of Peace. "I almost forgot to show you what found me today. Actually, we found each other. He reached into his pocket and pulled out Crystal. She really helped me today." He extended his hand to show her Crystal. "Isn't Crystal beautiful, Mom?"

58

"Yes, it is honey. Now go up and get washed up for dinner. Your dad will be home soon." David headed up to his room, leaving his mother in shock. She couldn't wrap her head around what David had told her.

At dinner, David told his dad about his experiences that day. Dad listened silently, his face expressionless. "Dad, what do you think about the Game I played with Love today? You don't seem excited by my story".

"David, I think you have an amazing imagination, and it seems you have had fun playing make-believe."

"Don't you believe that Love talked to me and that I saw Love everywhere?"

"David, I think you believe you did, but I would like to give it some deeper thought. We can talk about it later. I am glad that you are now acknowledging the existence of God. I was concerned yesterday after church when you were expressing doubts."

David's smile disappears, and he quietly says, "Okay, Dad." He finishes his dinner in silence and, exhausted, asks to be excused to go to his room.

After David went to his room, Dad shared his concerns. "I am worried that David might have some psychological issues. I fear that if David tells anyone that he sees God, Love, or whatever, and God is talking to him, he will be ridiculed as being crazy."

Mom says, "Yes, David might be ridiculed and even bullied if he told others. But what David experienced today seems to go way beyond imagination. How could he, on his own, create such a well-developed spiritual perspective after spending one day in the park?"

Dad responds, "It may be a well-developed perspective, but I can't accept it. It goes beyond my beliefs. It sounds like pagan or cult thinking."

Mom adds, "For me, it is a mind-boggling mystery. I want to support David, so let's see how it plays out.

David lays down on his bed and hears Love say, "I AM here."

David said, "I thought my dad would be happy for me that I saw you today."

"David, many people aren't ready to hear about what you experienced. They have rigid beliefs that resist the possibility that I could be heard or seen. Even though he may not act the way you would like, I AM your dad, too. The Love Game you played today never ends. If you keep your heart and eyes open, there is always more of me to discover. There are also more levels to the Game. Each level will be progressively more challenging. For example, the challenge of choosing to see Me in your Dad when he isn't responding the way you want. Or, choosing to see me hidden in Butch, the boy who bullies you, will take a higher level of awareness and commitment to playing the game."

"Thank you, God, for an amazing and fun day. I'll see you tomorrow." Then, with a sense of wonder and gratitude, David slipped into a peaceful sleep.

Mom came up to check on David and found him lying on the top of his bed, fast asleep. She covered him with a blanket and whispered in his ear, "I love you." She turned out the light, and as she was leaving, she heard a woman's voice say, "I AM here."

David's mom walks down the hall, thinking about the voice she just heard. She wonders if David's imagination is rubbing off on her. Suddenly, she remembers a time when she was a young child when she would hear voices. Her mother overheard her talking to someone who wasn't there and asked who she was talking to. She said that it was her friend. Her mother became very angry. She yelled at her to never speak of it again. She was told that it was the devil trying to get control of her mind. Her grandmother heard voices, and she was put in an insane asylum. Mom continued conversing with her friend for a little while after that. She didn't think her friend was telling her anything evil, but she became so afraid that someone would find out she asked her friend to leave her alone. She didn't hear from her friend again, at least until tonight.

Chapter 12

God as Love

Tuesday, June 11

"Wake up, David, it's time to play!"

"Good morning, Love," David says without opening his eyes. "Are we going to play the Love Game again today?"

"Maybe yes and maybe no, David. It is your choice at each moment. Let's see how the day unfolds."

David sat up in bed and was surprised to see that he still had his clothes on from yesterday. He gets up and goes to the kitchen. His mom smiles at him and says, "Good morning, sleepy head."

"Hey, mom. How come you didn't wake me so I could get ready? I didn't take a bath, brush my teeth, get into my pajamas, or even say my prayers."

"You were sleeping so peacefully I didn't want to disturb you. I thought your normal prayer seemed unnecessary and maybe inappropriate after the day you had had. Maybe it's time for you to create your own way to pray. For now, how about washing up and changing your clothes while I get your breakfast ready?"

David remembers he was going to meet Angela in the park today. He is excited to see her and tell her about his experiences. Unlike his Dad's response last night, he knew in his heart that she would enjoy hearing his story. David puts on clean play clothes and opens his bedroom door to get something to eat when he hears Crystal say, "Hey David, are you forgetting me?"

He turns around to see Crystal sitting on his desk. "I'm so sorry, I could never forget you. Would you like to come with me today?"

"I sure do." David put Crystal in his pocket and headed to the kitchen.

"Has Dad left for work yet?"

"Yes, he had to leave early today."

"Is Dad upset with me for what I told him yesterday?"

"No, honey, he is not upset with you. I think he is afraid. What you told him is so different from what he has been told about God and has come to believe as the truth that he is having trouble accepting your experience. He fears what others will think of you and how they will treat you." He wants the very best for you and doesn't want to see you hurt."

"I can accept that he is worried, Mom. You say he doesn't want to see me hurt, but does he know that I feel hurt when he fails to support me?"

"I know it doesn't seem to make sense to you now, but hopefully, you will find peace when someone acts in a way you don't like. Maybe Love has a perspective that will help you. Now, go ahead and eat your breakfast. Aren't you going to meet Angela in the park today?"

"I didn't tell you that I was meeting Angela."

"You must have. How would I have known?"

"I don't know, but I am sure I didn't tell you."

"Maybe I thought that since you had a special moment with her, you would want to see her again."

"You are right, Mom; I did have a special moment, and I hope to see her in the park today."

"What time are you meeting her?"

"I don't know. We didn't make any plans. Do you have anything like birdseed that I can take to Chickadee if I see her?"

"I think we might. Why don't you finish your breakfast, and I'll see what I can find."

David finished eating at about the same time his mom returned with a small bag of seeds. "Thanks a lot, Mom."

"You're welcome, honey; I love you. Have a wonderful day."

"Luv you too."

On his walk to the park, he thought about that expression: "I love you." He heard it from his mom, and it made him feel good. He always said it back to her, thinking it would make her feel good, too. He would find himself telling his mother he loved her when she did something nice for him. He doesn't remember anyone else, including his dad, saying the words to him. He wondered what "I love you" really meant. "Hey, Love, are you here?"

"Always, David. So, you want to know what 'I love you' means when your mom says it to you? Have you asked her what it means to her?"

"No, I haven't. And why doesn't my dad tell me he loves me? If he doesn't say it, does it mean that he doesn't love me?"

"You know David, I don't answer 'why' questions. You might ask your dad what the phrase "I love you" means to him. Tell him that you have noticed that he doesn't say it much, and you have been wondering if he doesn't feel good about you."

"Do you love me, God?"

"No, David. I do not."

"What? That's what I thought you do."

"I AM LOVE, I AM YOU, YOU ARE ME, YOU ARE LOVE. LOVE is. It is an 'Isness' that is always present and is unconditional and Perfect. When you ask, 'Do you love me?' you are thinking of Love as an action or something you do to another being or a pizza. But Love is not an action - it's what you are at your Divine core. It isn't something you do or give away - it is your true nature waiting to be uncovered. When you open your heart to this truth, Love will naturally radiate to everything and everyone without discrimination."

"Having said that, the actions you take when you have opened your heart to your Loveself may be seen as loving. For example, expressing appreciation to Cloud, hugging Tree, showing compassion to Angela, showing kindness to Mrs. Deera, nurturing Chick-a-dee, and caring for Crystal were all loving because your heart was open. It was also loving because you were not trying to manipulate them to get something in return. That includes seeking appreciation or validation."

David stops walking, looks up with his eyebrows furrowed as he tries to absorb Love's words. He had never thought about Love this way before but the Perfect feeling he is experiencing validates Love's message. After a short pause he resumes his walk to the park.

"Yesterday, you did something awesome, my precious One. You discovered the superpower that you have longed for – this is Love. It was like Clark Kent removing his clothes, which hid his Superman nature. You let go of your judgments that have covered up your Divine nature as Love. Your open heart activates your x-ray vision to see through an individual's masks of fear, beliefs, and suffering to reveal the Perfect Love that I AM. Awakening your heart to me allows your Loveself to shine brightly in all directions without selecting some beings and not others. Even if you're just looking in one direction or person, that Lovelight is so magical that it actually brightens the whole world."

"Wow, that sounds awesome. But yesterday, I lost that perfect feeling, my superpower, when I thought my dad didn't appreciate my experience. What happened?"

"You close your heart the moment your judgmental mind decides how a person should or shouldn't act or who or what should be loved or not. The beautiful thing is that you can open your heart to Love again and again when you allow your expectations or judgments to move on."

"Many believe love comes in shades and degrees, but the truth is, when Loveself blossoms, it does so fully and without hesitation. Consider the phrase "falling in love." It's often a dance of acceptance, a journey through personal barriers rather than an immediate dive into the heart's deepest embrace. It's possible to flip between experiencing the presence of love and not, countless times within a day - a testament to the inner tides of judgment that we navigate."

"When one claims to love another, it often reflects a state of joy within themselves - a mirror of their own well-being rather than comparative affection. Yet, true Love, the kind I embody, is unwavering and infinite. It doesn't wax and wane; it simply is."

Love continues: "You are an embodiment of this Love. Whether you realize it or not is up to you. And if another fails to recognize this Love within you, it's not for lack of its existence but rather their current inability to peel away the layers of judgment that cloud their vision."

"You don't have the power to make someone else see their own perfect, loving nature. However, you can choose to live with your heart wide open, to see the unblemished beauty in others, and to celebrate the perfection that they might yet have to discover within themselves."

David pipes up: "Oh, Love, there's Angela sitting on the bench where we met yesterday. David starts running toward her. "I'm really excited to see her again. Can we talk more about you later?"

"I AM always here."

Angela, with a big smile on her face, jumps up when she sees David coming.

"Hey, Angela, I'm glad you came back. They hug again, lasting longer than yesterday, each of them being less self-conscious about the physical contact. David says, "I see the Love that you are, and I really feel good, Angela."

"What a nice thing to say, David. I couldn't stop thinking about our time together yesterday. I have also been wondering if you saw God."

"I did, and I do right now."

"What do you mean? I don't see God."

"I see you as God, but I don't prefer the word God. Since God is Love, and I see you as Love, then I am seeing you as God."

"That's a lot to swallow. Maybe if you take some smaller steps and tell me about how the day went yesterday and how you were able to see Love."

Chapter 13

Angela and Chickadee

"Okay, I'll start with Mrs. Deera. She was the lady who was struggling to carry her groceries. Do you mind if we walk as we talk? I've got so much energy; I don't think I could sit still."

"That's fine with me, David. I, too, am excited."

As they walked, David recounted the story of Mrs. Deera.

"That's amazing how you knew all about her."

"I don't know how I knew about her. It just came out." Here is Chickadee's tree. Let's sit for a moment. I want to share something special with you."

They sit on the bench next to the tree, and David reaches into the bag his mom gave him and pulls out some seeds.

"Watch this, Angela," he says as he extends his hand with the seeds and calls out, "Hey Chickadee, I AM here." A few moments went by, and the tiny bird flew down and landed on David's fingertips. "Good morning, Chickadee. I brought some more food for you and your chicks."

"Thank you, David. Who is your friend?"

"This is Angela. I am showing her how I found Love yesterday,"

Chickadee looks directly into Angela's eyes. Angela was filled with a warm feeling unlike anything she had felt before. Chickadee then picked out a seed and flew up into the tree.

"Oh, my gosh, David. That was incredible."

David poured the rest of the seeds he was holding into the palm of Angela's hand. "Now it is your turn."

Angela hesitated for a brief moment. "I don't think I can do it."

"You might be right, or you might not be. You won't know if you just think about it without trying."

"I won't just think about it; I'll do it." She held out her hand with the seeds, and soon Chickadee flew down and landed on her fingertips. Angela's eyes opened wide in surprise. She again looked into Chickadee's eyes and felt another surge of warm energy flow through her body.

Chickadee selected a seed and flew back up into the tree.

"When she comes back, talk to her, Angela, and then listen with your heart."

"How do I listen with my heart, David?"

David repeats to Angela just what Love told him yesterday. It didn't take long before Chickadee returned. Angela raised her hand closer to her face until Chickadee was not more than a foot away.

"You are so beautiful, Chickadee. Thank you for sitting in my hand. I can see how David found Love here. David said you have chicks. How are they doing?"

"They are changing every day, Angela. They appreciate the seeds you are providing. It won't be long before they fly down and eat by themselves. For now, I enjoy caring for them and feeding them. My chicks are a lot like you two. Their survival depends on the love of someone else to provide a nest and food for them to grow and learn the ways of Love. The survival game is what every being on earth plays. Some people learn to play the Love Game and

68

discover their true Nature. That's the game David played yesterday, and you are now beginning, Angela. My job is to teach my chicks how to follow their Nature and appreciate the joy of being."

Chickadee took another seed and flew back to her nest before Angela could ask any more questions.

"Oh my God, David, did you hear that? "

"What? I didn't hear anything. If Chickadee spoke to you, it would be through your heart. I wouldn't hear what is in your heart unless it spoke to my heart at the same time."

After Angela told David what Chickadee said, she looked down and was startled to see a squirrel sitting near her feet. "Hi, I'm Angela, and this is David."

"Hi, I am Squirrel. Chickadee told me that Love was offering some seeds here. I came to see for myself."

"We have some seeds for you." Angela pours the rest of the seeds in her hand on the ground near Squirrel." David and Angela watch as Squirrel stuffs his cheeks with seeds and then scampers off.

"Doesn't that make your heart sing, Angela?"

"Did you hear what the Squirrel say about Love offering seeds?"

Angela nodded.

David continued, "He was talking about us as Love. That is what I meant when I told you that I see the Love that you are."

"I AM here."

Angela looks around and then toward David. "Who said that?"

David responds, "That there was the voice of Love."

Love then says, "The beings around can sense your Divine Light radiating from your open heart."

Initially, tears of Joy filled Angela's eyes, but then an electricity unlike anything she had ever experienced surged up and down her spine. Fear of this uncontrollable force overwhelmed her, and she started sobbing.

"What's wrong, David asks?" She couldn't stop crying long enough to answer,

A part of him wanted to hug her and comfort her, to make her feel better. He just didn't know what was happening.

"I AM here, David. Angela's tears are an expression of the intensity of her feelings right now. Everything is Perfect."

"What can I do, Love?"

"I invite you to keep your heart open and be present as you were yesterday when you first met Angela. Your actions are your choice." David decides to take Love's suggestion but he also chooses to move a little closer to Angela. He feels a deep connection to her.

Angela's crying subsides a little, and she looks up into David's eyes. This triggered more crying. David still sat quietly. Chickadee flies down, sits on the arm of the bench, and says, "I AM here too."

Finally able to say a few words, Angela uttered, "I am so sorry, David. I have never felt this. I have to leave right now. I'm so sorry."

"Would you like for me to walk with you?"

"No, David. Not now. I have to go home." Tears rolling down her cheeks, Angela takes off.

Chapter 14

The Survival Game

David's perfect feeling was gobbled up in thoughts and judgments. He felt let down and sad. "Hey Love, what just happened?" His heart was quiet. "Love, are you here?" Still, no answer. "Love, have you left me too?"

He remembered that he put Crystal in his pocket. Maybe she could help him understand. He reached in and pulled her out. "Crystal, I don't know what just happened. Everything seemed to be going well with Angela, but she suddenly wanted to leave. The feeling of rejection that I have experienced many times before came right up to the surface. What's wrong with me, Crystal?"

The lovely stone responds: "That seems to be an important question for you. What would Peace Pond say?"

"I imagine that Peace Pond would invite me to focus on my breath to help bring me into the present moment. Okay, Crystal, I get your point." David closes his eyes and focuses on his breath. He imagines himself looking into Peace Pond.

He starts by throwing the question, "What's wrong with me?" into the pond. Then, with each breath, he allows his thoughts about the question's answer to also flow into the pond. He steps into the pond and notices how calm the muscles in his legs become. He takes another step further into the pond. The calmness rises and continues to do so until he is fully immersed in the water.

"I AM here, David."

"There's nothing wrong with you. Angela's first experience with Divine Love surprised and scared her. She is doing the best she can to care for herself.

If you are concerned, you can follow her to her home and check on her. What Angela experienced was perfect. Now it is up to you to decide whether you want to continue playing the Love Game or not."

"I don't know."

"What are you afraid of?"

"Maybe she doesn't want to see me, and that would hurt."

"Are you trying to predict the future? I don't even do that. Come back to the present moment. Allow your heart to move your body."

David opens his eyes and starts running in the direction that Angela went. He doesn't slow down until he sees Angela go into a house. He stops to catch his breath and remembers what Love told him. Angela's experience was perfect for her at that moment. He wonders if choosing to accept that Love knows is what faith is all about. Also, if this experience was perfect for Angela, it must be perfect for him. That means there are gifts in the process of being unwrapped. He decides to keep his heart and eyes open. "Let's go home, Crystal?"

***

Angela runs up the stairs into her bedroom and flops on her bed. Her heart was still pounding from the run home. She relives the experiences with the chickadee, squirrel, and David. Nana knocks on her door.

"Are you OK, Angela?"

"Yes, Nana, I don't want to talk right now. I'm really tired."

"Ok, I'll give you some space. Let me know if I can help."

"Thanks, Nana."

Hey, Love, are you here?"

"I AM, Angela."

"Thanks, Love, for coming when I called. I have so many questions. To start with, what happened to me in the park? What made me start shaking as if I had been shocked? Is this my cancer or something else?"

"Angela, dear, I AM always here for you. You had a physical reaction to my presence. Sometimes, the energy of Love can surge through your nervous system like electricity. This unfamiliar energy was so intense that it triggered thoughts of fear. There is nothing wrong with you and definitely nothing to be afraid of."

"I'm not sure how to talk to Nana about what happened. I'm concerned she won't understand, or she will just think I'm crazy. Should I keep it a secret from Nana?"

"I don't dispense should's or shouldn'ts, Angela. These are future dependent. I AM present in the now, and anything I might suggest is for this present moment. Your choice as to what to tell Nana will depend on whether you choose to play the Love Game or the fear-focused survival game. Either way, what you do will be perfect."

"OK, Love, then what do you suggest at this present moment?"

"What would bring you happiness right now?"

"Probably to draw my experience with David today."

"Do I need to say anything more, my dear Angela?"

***

On the walk home, David wonders if what just happened with Angela could hold some gift for him. That was topped off by the thought that Love had abandoned him. He is unsettled when he is uncertain and doesn't understand what is happening. David likes to know things and asks a lot of "why" questions. Love refuses to answer "why" questions. His parents frequently answer why questions with "because

I say so," especially when he is asked to do something he doesn't want to do.

"Hey, Love, I know you don't answer 'why' questions, but there was a moment when I thought you abandoned me. I felt sad, confused, and a little scared when Angela left. I thought I had done something wrong, and she didn't want to be around me anymore. I asked you what happened, and you didn't answer. What about now? What happened?"

"In that moment, you were experiencing those emotions, you closed your heart and muffled my voice. You shifted to playing the survival game. Remember, we are One, and I never go away. You cover me up when your imagination takes you into a world of fear—focusing your attention on something you don't want to happen. It becomes your momentary reality. Your frightened emotional response is just a product of the story you tell yourself. Your story creates your reality or what you believe is true. Although we are all one, people separate themselves, each creating their own unique world of reality by the stories they tell."

"What is the survival game, Love?"

"The survival game is a competitive self-care game that humans play with other people as well as with other animals and just about everything that exists on earth. The game's premise is based on people's belief that there is not enough of what they desire or need to go around for everyone. So, you must compete for what you want. You compete for love, respect, security, wealth, power, health, happiness, value, and even time. In this game, you get to create your own reality and experience a wide range of emotions."

"How do I win this game?"

"The goal of the survival game is getting what you want. The strategy is to avoid or fight what you don't want. It is a game where you win or lose, succeed or fail. There is an underlying fear of not getting what you want or failing. This game depends on rules and judgments, rewards, and punishments. Power to influence the actions of others is valued, whether that be through manipulation or force. Although not outwardly acknowledged as good, lying to get what you want is a pervasive part of the game. Ultimately, it is a self-care game that focuses on your physical, emotional, or spiritual well-being. You lose the game when you think you have lost or your physical form dies.

"What is the difference between the two games?"

"Here are a few differences, David. In the Love Game, you focus on appreciating what you have at the moment. Mystery and uncertainty are embraced. Everything is seen as perfect, and everyone wins. There are no victims. You play the Love Game with your heart.

In the survival game, you focus on what you lack and how to get it in the future. You play this game with your conditioned mind or ego. Uncertainty is an enemy. Everything in the survival game is seen as imperfect, with people striving to be less imperfect. Many who play this game may identify themselves as victims. Productivity is honored, but being non-productive is a burden. Both games have value."

"Love, shouldn't I always try to play the Love Game instead of the survival game? It seems that the survival game is going to cause me distress?"

"David, it is more valuable for you to learn the answer to that question through experience. One of the reasons your soul incarnated into your body is to have the opportunity to play the survival game. Playing that game allows you to experience the world of thoughts, a full spectrum of emotions, physical sensations, and even desires. With these experiences, you have the opportunity to learn and create while serving the Oneness. Your choices in this life can make a difference to the well-being of all."

"David, one moment you might be playing the Love Game, and the next moment you may find yourself playing the survival game. The beauty of these games is that you will create your own world reality with either one you choose to play."

David reaches home and is greeted by Mom. "How was your day?"

"It wasn't the way I expected it to turn out." He tells his mom about Angela and her reaction to hearing and seeing Love. He is still confused about her response. His mom listens without offering her opinions.

"What do you think happened, Mom? I hope it isn't something that I did."

"I really don't know. Maybe she was afraid of something. I'm sure everything will work out."

David was hesitant to talk about the survival game. He wasn't confident that he understood the game enough to talk about it clearly. His hesitancy comes from a fear that what he would tell her about what he learned from Love would be rejected. It would be rejected not because of the truth of the message but because he would botch it up when he tried to explain it. He thought he would wait until he understood more about that game.

"Hey, David, Love interjects. I am here to remind you that understanding is overrated. It isn't necessary."

"OK, Love. I guess I was playing the survival game when I was concerned that what I learned from you might be rejected, especially if I didn't say it in the right way. I have always worried that I would be misunderstood and judged by what I say."

"Yes, David, you are playing the survival game in those moments of worry. That is something to notice but not judge."

At that moment, Tippy, the family dog, nestles up to David. He thinks that Tippy is the only one other than Love that really accepts him. "I'm going outside to play with Tippy," he tells his mom. He enjoys wrestling and running with this big, gentle dog. He realized while playing how much he liked touching and being touched. Other than getting hugs from his mom and dad, he doesn't get touched much. He then recalled all the times he experienced the touch of Love over the last day. His mom, Tree, Angela, Mrs. Deera, Chickadee, Crystal, and Peace Pond all touched him, and now Tippy. Even walking in the grass barefoot made him happy. You can't touch something and not be touched. His thoughts about touch get interrupted by the sound of his mom's voice yelling out the back door.

"Time for dinner, David."

The conversation at dinner that evening revolved around what was going on with his dad and work. David was typically quiet at the dinner table and only talked when he

76

was asked a question. Then he talked and talked until he was asked to stop.

The family had just finished their dinner and were still sitting at the table when David asked, "Mom and Dad, is it okay if I ask you two a couple of questions that Love suggested that I ask you?" after a brief pause, "Remember Dad, Love is what I call God."

David's dad turned his eyes toward mom without moving his head with a slight furrow in his brow. "I suppose so. Go ahead."

"Mom, what do you mean when you say the words 'I love you'? And Dad, I have noticed that you rarely say it to me. Does that mean you don't love me?"

Then, looking in Mom's direction, David asked, "Mom, I hate it when you are angry and yell at me or try to hurt me with the paddle. How can you love me and want to hurt me at the same time? I really want to feel safe around you, but I don't. When I sense that you are upset about something, I stay away. You say that I just have to obey you so you won't get angry. Does that mean you will love me only if I act the way you want me to? My survival and safety depend on pleasing you two and other adults as well. I feel that I must keep everyone happy if I want to be accepted and loved. That paddle hanging on the wall is a reminder. Is that what you want? Do you want me to be responsible for your love and happiness?"

There was an uncomfortable silence as David and Michael waited for Mom and Dad's response.

Mom's voice quivered, "I don't know what to say." She took a sip of water and cleared her throat. "Give me time to think about your questions."

David senses their discomfort and says, "I know I just sprung these questions on you. It's okay if you don't answer me now, but I hope to talk to you sometime soon.

Michael chimes in, "I would also be interested in your response to David's questions."

Mom says, "I think both of you boys deserve an answer. We can arrange some uninterrupted time to talk about it later. Right now, I want to clean up the kitchen and give Tom a bath before he goes to bed."

Dad then follows, "Yes, David, I, too, would like some time alone with you without distractions. Although it is a little awkward for me to talk about it, I think it is time to reflect more deeply on the question, not just for you alone but for myself, your mom, and your brothers."

"That would be great. Let me know when you are ready." David jumps up to start clearing the dishes from the table and sets them on the counter by the sink. Tonight is his time to wash the dishes. Michael will dry them and put them away. Dad goes to his office, and Mom takes Tom upstairs. "David," says Michael, "I can't believe you had the guts to ask Mom and Dad those questions, but I'm sure glad you did."

"I just had to know, Michael."

David's thoughts shift. He thinks about what Love told him about creating reality. He is very skeptical that he could be making what is happening in his life. If he had control, he wouldn't be doing the dishes. "Michael, Love told me that each of us creates our own reality. I don't understand that at all. Do you?"

"I don't know how we could. I don't think I have control over anything, especially as a kid. For example, neither of us wants to be doing the dishes. Complaining doesn't help, and refusing to do them has consequences. Let's get them done as fast as possible. Let me know if you find out how we create our reality."

They finish the dishes and head to their bedrooms.

Chapter 15

Creating Reality

David lays down on his bed and calls out, "Hey, Love, I can't see how I am creating my reality. I don't think I have much control over my life. My parents are making the decisions for me."

"What are you feeling right now?"

"I'm feeling happy that you are speaking to me."

"Did you ask for your parent's permission to talk to me?"

"Of course not."

"Then you are telling me that what you are experiencing at this moment is something you created yourself."

"I guess so. But you are here. You made me happy."

"And where is here?"

"Inside me and everywhere."

"Did I make you appreciate me? Did I control your thoughts? No. You made a choice to open your heart to my invitation to play the Love Game, to see the world through my eyes. You created the reality of your happiness. You are the creator of your reality."

"If you want to be happy, create it now. It comes from inside you, not from external conditions meeting your requirements. That means that you alone are responsible for your happiness."

You may choose to relinquish your power to be happy now, waiting for the right person, the right moment, or the right situation in the future. You might delay your happiness until your favorite football team wins the Superbowl. Or you might choose to live your life as a victim by putting your happiness in the hands of someone else who wants to control you. Every experience has value and can inspire creativity. But if happiness is important to you, start by appreciating whatever you have at this moment."

David nods. "Fine, I see how appreciation may result in feeling happy. I still don't know how I create the reality of what I see or hear, is happening around me or to me."

"Most people think reality is what is before them that they can experience objectively with their five senses. Each person creates their own reality from the way they make meaning out of what they are sensing. This meaning is based on their beliefs, memories, and the stories that others tell. You may tell the story that you don't have any say about what you are allowed to do or not. Many people feel that way their entire lives. You do have control over what you choose to think and what you choose to believe or not. You have control over what you accept or reject. You have control over which game you want to play. And you have the power to choose how you use your imagination. You may not have control over situations that occur in your life or those around you, but I have gifted you with the power to create your own reality about how you view and experience those situations. It's your gift. No one can take it from you without your permission."

"Maybe I'm confused about what creation is. The Bible says you created everything in six days, and you rested the seventh. Does that mean that all creations were finished in that week, and you haven't created anything since? Am I really creating anything new?"

"That is a story some people tell and others don't, David. What I created is creators. You are a creator, as Nature itself is a creator. Creation has never stopped. Each change, each death, and each birth becomes a new creation."

David counters. "You mean you don't control if someone like Angela gets cancer or not? Or if she lives or dies?"

"I AM not a puppet master controlling lives. You are the master of yourself! Some of your creations are intentional, and some go on behind the scenes almost automatically. Your own body is recreating new versions of itself every moment. Creation is inspired by both suffering and joy. The Universe continues to change, but the Love that I AM that connects all existence to Oneness is Constant. That includes everything in the physical realm that you can experience with your five senses as well as those aspects of the spiritual existence that you may perceive with your non-ordinary senses."

"I don't understand why anyone would create suffering for themselves."

"Asking for understanding is like asking a 'why' question in disguise."

"You can inquire, and you or someone else may give you an explanation that makes sense to you, but you'll never fully grasp the entire truth. It's like trying to understand a whole puzzle by looking only at one piece."

"Your world is nothing more than a playground for your soul and others to experience a physical form with a diversity of emotions and desires. It allows souls to witness and appreciate the fruits of creativity."

"You can create your life experiences out of love or out of fear. Your thoughts and desires reflect your focus. The desire shows you where you want to go, and your feelings reflect the focus of your thoughts. If the thoughts point in the opposite direction of what you desire, your desires will never be fulfilled."

"Fear isn't bad, and you may want to focus on it in order to have the experience it offers. But if you desire a different experience, then you will need to adjust your thoughts to align with your desires. Your feelings are your greatest gift, David. Appreciate them like a compass. For example, consider the situation where the feelings you desire are in the North, but your compass says your thoughts are facing unwanted feelings in the South. This awareness offers you an opportunity to choose. Stay with your thoughts focused on unwanted feelings, or turn your thoughts in the direction of what you want in the North. You will never get to the north pole walking south.

"I can imagine, Love, that the journey of some people who want to go north would land at the south pole."

"Yes, David. At that point if they keep moving, their next step can only be to the north. Can you remember a time when your focus and desire were pointing in opposite directions?"

"I guess that would be any time I'm fearful about not getting what I want. I want to be accepted by others but I worry that they won't. I am not happy because I fear that other people will reject me or even hurt me physically. I end up keeping a distance from others and not engaging with them. Is there value in being unhappy?"

"There is value in everything. Experiencing unhappiness may inspire you to shift your perspective, such as choosing to play the Love Game instead of the survival game. It might draw you to making connections with others for their assistance. It may expand your resources for self-care. As you learn how to appreciate the moment and create your happiness within, you will have more empathy and compassion in service to others who are suffering."

"I want to be happy, but how can I be," David asks, "when I AM made to do things I don't want to do or when people want to hurt me?"

"Flood your mind with appreciation. There is no happiness without appreciation. Find the perfection of the moment, accept the now as it is, use your imagination, and tell a story of Love. Go to the Peace Pond. If you have difficulty turning away from your unhappiness, Ask for help. I AM here."

"The next time you do the dishes, see if you can find a way to be happy with the opportunity. It's also OK if you aren't happy in this lifetime because this lifetime isn't the end."

82

"Love, I am feeling tired. I am going to go to bed and create a dream world. Thanks for being here for me."

"I AM here and always will be. David."

David's mom comes in. "Are you ready for bed yet?

"Yes, Mom, I just finished brushing my teeth."

"Did you say your prayers?"

"No, I don't need to. I've been talking to Love all day. I think my life is a prayer."

"Well then, good night and sweet dreams. I love you, and I will tell you more about what that means to me tomorrow."

Chapter 16

Nana's Secret

Wednesday, June 12

"Wake up, David. It's time to play."

"Wonderful, Love."

Immediately, David thinks of Angela and wonders how she is doing. He will go to her house to check on her later.

At breakfast, his mom was quieter than usual. David wonders if she was thinking of the question he asked. He decided not to ask again. He tells her that he is going to Angela's house to see how she is doing.

David is nervous, clenching his fists as he walks up the steps of her porch. He rings the bell, and a few moments later, Angela's grandmother answers.

"Hi, I'm David. Is Angela here?"

"I AM Nana Sage, David. Angela hasn't come out of her room yet. I think she may still be sleeping."

"I was wondering how she was feeling today."

"Aren't you the boy Angela told me about to who talks with God?"

"Yes. I was with Angela yesterday when she started crying."

"What happened? Did you do something to her, David?"

"I didn't do anything to her. Did Angela say that I did?"

"No, she wouldn't tell me what was wrong or what happened. She went up to her room and continued crying for a long time. I tried to comfort her, but she wanted to be left alone. Now sit down with me on the porch and tell me what happened to upset Angela.

David recounted the story of him meeting her and telling her how he talked to Love, that is, God, and saw Love in many places, including how he saw Love as Angela.

"I wanted to show her how she could see and hear Love, so I introduced her to Chickadee. That is a little bird I met yesterday. I showed Angela how to feed Chickadee by putting a few seeds into her hand. Chickadee flew down and landed on Angela's fingertips. She talked to Chickadee before the little bird took a seed and flew back to her nest. I didn't hear what Chickadee told her because she was talking to Angela's heart, not mine. Angela was smiling and was enjoying the experience. Next, a squirrel showed up at her feet, and she gave the squirrel a few seeds. I did hear what Squirrel told her. He was speaking to the both of us. The squirrel left, and that's when Love spoke to her and me. Our hearts heard, "I AM Here." She didn't know who said it, but I told her it was Love. That's what I call God. I AM here is what Love says when it wants to remind me of Love's presence. Tears of joy filled Angela's eyes. Then Love went on to tell us that all the beings around us can sense that we have uncovered our true nature and the light of Love is pouring out of our hearts." Angela said she started to experience an intense energy surging up and down her body, and I noticed she was shaking. She became really afraid and started to cry hard. She said she had to go home right away. I tried to help, but she ran home."

Nana Sage says, "Now I understand what happened. Angela felt the Spirit of God touch her. This can be an intense and powerful experience. She may feel she is losing

86

control or going crazy. This can be very frightening. I will talk to her and let her know she is ok."

David says, "I haven't had that kind of experience with Love?"

"Not everyone has that physical experience, and it doesn't mean that your experience with Love is not just as valuable."

"Nana, have you had a physical experience like Angela's?"

"Yes, I have. It first happened to me when I was about Angela's age, and I was playing alone in the woods. I didn't tell anyone because I didn't want them to think of me as crazy. Later, I witnessed people having weird physical gyrations in church. I was told they were being touched by the spirit of the Lord, and that was a good thing. It happened to me a couple of other times when I was by myself. I still was too embarrassed to talk about it. In fact, you are the first person I have ever told."

"Thank you. It means a lot to me that you feel safe telling me something so personal."

"I AM here."

"Did you hear that, Nana Sage?"

"Yes, I did," Nana Sage said with a big smile on her face.

"What a Perfect day for Love, Nana Sage."

"Yes, yes, yes, David. But then again, every day is a Perfect day for Love."

"Please tell Angela that I was here and that I will come by tomorrow if she wants to play."

"I appreciate that you came today. I will let Angela know. It was nice meeting you, David. I'm sure I will be seeing more of you. Bye."

David felt satisfied and decided to go home instead of playing in the park.

When Angela came out from her bedroom, Nana Sage told her to get some cereal, and afterward, they needed to talk. Angela had a glass of orange juice and a bowl of Cheerios, then joined Nana on the porch. That was Nana's favorite place to talk.

"David came by this morning to see how you were feeling. He told me a little about what happened yesterday from his perspective. Would you like to talk to me now about what you experienced?"

"I don't know Nana. You might think there is something wrong with me."

"Let me tell you, child, about something that I experienced when I was about your age. The only other person that I have ever told was David. I, too, was afraid to tell anyone out of fear that they would think I was crazy."

She told Angela the story of how she was alone in the woods, sitting by a stream. "I lost all sense of time and suddenly had a feeling that I was one with all of nature. I was floating above the forest and could see my house in the distance and the animals in the woods so clearly. I could even see myself sitting by the stream. Then I rose higher, and I could see the whole county. Everything was beautiful and perfect. I don't know how long this lasted. When I started to come back down and reunite with my body, I started shaking. There was an intense surge of energy moving up and down my spine. Even though it wasn't painful, I thought something terrible was happening. It didn't last long. By the time I walked out of the woods and back home, I felt better. I decided to keep it to myself. In church, I saw a woman shaking during the service. No one paid her any mind, but I thought she had a bug crawling down her dress, and I started to laugh. My momma shushed me and told me the lady was being touched by the Spirit of God. I then assumed that was what had happened to me. I had the experience a couple more times when I was alone, but I was never afraid of feeling it again. I didn't tell anyone after that because I thought it was supposed to be a private thing between me and God.

"Oh, Nana, what you described was a lot like what happened to me. Thanks for telling me. I don't feel like I'm alone."

"David said that a Chickadee was eating out of your hand, and she talked to you."

"Yes, and it was absolutely amazing. David said the bird doesn't actually talk with words, but it sends a message to my heart. If I have an open heart, then I will be able to translate the message into words that I can understand."

"By the way, David says he is going to come by in the morning if you want to play with him."

"Nana, I felt so bad for him yesterday. He didn't know what was happening, and I would really like to go back to the park with him tomorrow."

"Honey, he seems like a very nice boy, and I can see why you like him."

"I do really like him. He is different from any boy I've met before, and I have that perfect feeling that reflects my Love for myself. I am excited to see him tomorrow."

***

When David arrives home, his mom says, "You're home early, How's Angela?"

"I met her grandmother, Nana Sage, and she told me Angela was still sleeping. I told her what had happened before Angela started crying, and Nana Sage said she understood what Angela had experienced. She thought Angela's reaction was from being touched by the Spirit of God. Nana said she would talk to Angela about that."

"I wondered that too, David. On a different subject, would you like to talk about the question you asked last night? I have given it a lot of thought."

"Yes, I would, Mom."

Chapter 17

Mom's Story

"What do I mean when I tell you that I love you? Do I want you to fear me? Do I love you when I am hurting you? Those are the questions I have been focused on since you asked me yesterday. To answer these questions, I want to give you a little background about my life."

"I was raised in a family where love was not expressed. I never heard those words from my mother or father. On the contrary, my mother was more apt to verbally cut me down or take a switch to me. A switch is a branch that she cut from a tree or bush. My father was gone much of the time, working two jobs. My brothers had more lenient rules than I had. One of my younger brothers would push me around or try to hurt me, and he was never punished for the way he treated me. I reached my limit when I was 13 and left home to be on my own. No one tried to stop me. That is two years older than you are now. I only got through eighth grade. I didn't think I was worth much then, and I still struggle with feeling inferior to people with more education. No matter what compliments I get for the good things I have done, it has never been enough to overcome my feelings of being less worthy. I worked hard and learned how to survive by reading people and taking care of their needs."

"The first time I experienced love was when I met Michael's father. I got married when I was 16. I thought I was in love when we first met because I felt appreciated for the first time in my life. I got pregnant right away. When Michael was born and I saw him for the first time, I was overwhelmed by a flood of beautiful feelings. As time passed, I realized Michael's father was a physically abusive alcoholic, and any feelings of "love" disappeared. We got divorced, and I was thrown back into trying to survive again, but this time, it wasn't just me that I had to protect. It was your brother."

"I moved back to the area where my parents lived so they could take care of your brother when I wasn't around. You think I abandoned you; I also abandoned your brother many times. The guilt has been so heavy on my heart that it just reinforced my unworthiness for love. Eventually, I met your father and once again felt appreciated and cared for, and felt hope that this love would last. I felt good that I could finally have your brother live with your dad and me. That was until your father started physically abusing him. He couldn't accept him as his son. It broke my heart, but I had to send your brother back to my parents for his own safety."

"I was so angry with your father, and whatever love feelings I had waned. But by that time, I was pregnant with you and had to consider your well-being. My basic needs were being taken care of, so I didn't leave him."

"I carried and nurtured you in my belly for nine months. Even though our bodies were separated at your birth, I still felt a powerful force still connecting us. It was an indescribable feeling. I told you that I loved you the first time I looked into your eyes. You were so innocent and beautiful and held me in such a way my feelings of inadequacy, insecurity, and worthlessness temporarily disappeared. I actually liked myself when I was holding you and singing to you."

"Wow, said David, "I remember some of those times and the songs you sang to me."

"Your first couple of years were complicated by illnesses, hospitalizations and surgeries. When you were about a year and a half old, you developed pneumonia and had to be hospitalized. It was so severe doctors didn't know whether you would survive. I had never experienced fear as intense as I did then thinking about losing you."

"There were a couple of incidents where your father was unusually rough with you. I had to get away, so once again. Your father didn't object to the divorce and he didn't have any desire to see you again. I don't think it was because of you but his desire to be free to pursue other women."

David hung his head, impressed by her story's gravity.

"I was a single mom with two sons to support. I worked two jobs and depended on babysitters when I was working. I was not interested in pursuing any other relationships, considering the bad choices that I had made in men before. All my energy focused on how I could keep you and your brother safe. The connection I felt for you two boys is what I call love. My fear of losing that connection took me out of love and sometimes into anger or rage. l was afraid I wasn't a good mother. I felt it was my job to prepare you for the world by teaching you what I thought was right and wrong based on my experience of trying to survive. I became afraid when you didn't obey me or acted in some way contrary to what I believed was right. I thought I had to control you to keep you safe. The only way I knew to do that was by punishing you.

David grimaced.

In moments where I lost control of my fear or anger, I would lash out and hurt you. In that moment, any love in my heart was covered with fear and rage. But the moment afterward when I saw you crying, hurt, and terrified, I was overcome by guilt and self-loathing. Memories of being beaten as a child came to the surface."

"I realized right away when I met your stepfather that he was a kind and gentle man. I watched him with critical eyes when you and your brother were with him. I noticed how he connected to you two. He treated me in a way that was

93

unlike any way I had ever been treated. I started to understand what love was with him. In moments where I felt this love, I felt good about myself. I attributed this to him and how he treated me, but I don't think that was it as I think about it now. It was when I was with him that I opened my heart to loving, appreciating, and accepting myself. He reflected love back to me. You do the same thing, David when I'm not worrying about you."

"I felt confident when I married him that he would care for you and your brother like you two were his biological sons. Every day, I feel so much gratitude for him bringing our family together. "

"I want you to know that I never want you to be afraid of me again. I will throw the paddle away and talk to you more if I get afraid."

"Does that mean I can climb trees?"

"Do you know why I am so afraid when you climb trees?"

"You probably worry that I will get hurt."

"Do you remember when you fell out of the tree in the back?"

"Sure, but I didn't think you knew."

"Mr. O'Brian, next door, saw you climb the big tree in the back. He was amazed that you could get so close to the top. That is when he heard a snap and saw you crash into one limb after another until you hit the ground. He knew there were a lot of logs on the ground. He thought for sure you would be dead. He took a step to check on you, but to his surprise, you jumped up immediately and walked into the woods. He called me right after that to tell me what happened. The thought of how you might have died scared me so much that when I imagined you had been climbing again, I went into a rage, reacting to my survival instincts and desire to avoid feeling the grief of losing you. At that moment, love was covered up."

Mom took a breath and went on. "When I tell you 'I love you,' it means that I'm grateful that you are in my life. It means that I feel a strong connection to you, and your wellbeing is of utmost importance to me. And it means that I am here for you."

94

"I want to protect you, keep you safe, nurture your well-being, and prepare you to survive on your own someday. I think of you as an extension of myself. What happens to you happens to me. If you are sick, I feel sick. When you fall and skin your knee, I feel the pain. When you are rejected by kids and feel sad, I do too. When you go to bed or leave the house, I tell you I love you to soothe you and remind you that I am here for you. I feel the same way about your brothers."

"Do you need me to tell you 'I Love you' back after you tell me?"

"Sometimes it is nice to hear you say that you Love me. Everyone wants to be appreciated and loved, and hearing the words feels good. Saying you love me out of habit takes away some of that good feeling compared to when you spontaneously, without reason, tell me that you love me."

"Mom, I see the Love that you are, and I feel Perfect." I don't have to Love you because you are Love. You may not accept what I'm saying yet, but you will when you can open your heart to accept yourself. In the moments you are feeling Love's presence for me, your heart is open to your own Loveself. Rejoice."

Chapter 18

Facing Fear

Thursday, June 13

"Wake up, Angela. It's time to play".

"Love, is that you?"

"Yes, it is? Are you surprised? I AM inviting you to play the next level of the Love Game."

"Do you think I'm ready? I don't know if I've got the first Level down yet."

"You don't have to be an expert at looking for me in things you feel connected to, enjoy, and appreciate. Remembering to play the Love Game is unending. You can still expand your ability to open your heart to your Loveself in more challenging situations by moving on to Level 2. Remember, the purpose of the Love Game is to experience and know me."

"What do I need to do for Level 2?"

"I would like you to go to the Peace Pond in the park. Once there, I will give you further instructions."

"I don't know where the Peace Pond is. I've never been there."

"I'll give you some directions."

"Should I write these down?"

"Should? No, My Angel Angela, you don't need to. Here are four steps to fulfilling your desire."

"First, clarify what you desire. In this case, it is to go to the Peace Pond."

"Second, walk in the direction of the Peace Pond. You don't need to know exactly where it is. You know it is part of the park, so start by facing it in that direction. Take a step."

"Third, listen with your heart and keep your eyes open. Sound familiar so far? Pay attention to the feelings that come from satisfying thoughts. Feelings and intuition will guide you."

"Fourth, if you have unwanted thoughts or undesired feelings, change the direction you are walking until you feel better. You may or may not get there walking a straight line, but deviations from the path may offer you valuable gifts. As always, I AM here."

"Wait. What is intuition?"

"Wait? I'm not going anywhere. Intuition is knowing something without knowing how you know it. It can be from your Loveself or from the spirit world such as those souls who have chosen to watch over you."

Angela gets dressed and eats breakfast. And tells Nana she is going to the Peace Pond.

Nana asks, "Do you know how to get there?"

"Love tells me I don't need to know. I just need to start walking. Love says, "Listen to your heart and keep your eyes open. Your feelings and intuition will guide you.""

"Well, that sounds like an adventure. Have fun, Angela,"

Angela heads toward the park, walking down the sidewalk. She wonders what level 2 of the Love Game is all about. She walks down a drive into one of the park's parking lots. From there, she follows a main path that leads deeper into the park. She stops at a fork in the path. She thinks, 'what now?'

"Hey, Love, what direction do I take to get to the pond?"

"What do your feelings tell you, Angela?"

98

"I don't have feelings one way or the other."

"Then it doesn't matter. Both directions offer gifts for your journey."

Angela takes the left fork and walks toward a wooded area of the park she has not been in before. She comes to a side path that would take her deeper into the woods. Something called her to take that way. Angela hesitated when she had a surge of fear. Hey Love, I would like some help. I'm hearing two voices. One is telling me to take that side path, and the voice of fear is telling me not to. Which one do I listen to?"

"Tell me more about your feelings."

"I'm excited about taking the side path. Fear is telling me that I may be making a mistake and something bad might happen if I go that way, and it would be safer to stay on the bigger, more traveled path."

"Is that a satisfying thought and feeling, Angela? When fear speaks, it is helpful to take a moment to assess the situation. In this present moment, are you in danger? Is there a bear standing in your way?"

"No." "What about making a mistake?

"What does making a mistake mean to you?"

"It means I went the wrong way, which may have led me away from my desire to get to the pond."

"From my perspective, mistakes are not bad. They're like feelings and reflect what's happening in the present moment. Both feelings and mistakes give you valuable information about what adjustments you could choose to make. In the Love Game, everything happens in the present moment, is Perfect and has value. If you aren't getting what you want, your focus is off-target. For example, if you shot an arrow at a target and it flew past the target on the left. It tells you to aim a little more to the right. It was not a mistake; it just provided you information about what adjustments you need to make to hit your target. When fear spoke, did you stop listening to your heart or close your eyes?"

"I might have."

"Did you see the sign by the tree next to the side path?"

"No, I didn't. I was looking at how the path narrowed, and it seemed to be darker down the path."

"Look now. What does the sign say?"

"It says Peace Pond with an arrow pointing down the path."

"Does that help you decide? Are you still afraid of going that way?"

"Thanks, Love."

Angela follows a winding path through some dense woods. She notices a lot of life happening around her. Birds chirping, squirrels scurrying, bees gathering pollen, and a parade of ants. Then her heart jumps when she sees a garter snake that she almost stepped on. She didn't know which way to turn.

"Love, help! There is a snake. I'm afraid of snakes. Maybe this is why I feared taking this path. Something told me I might encounter something as scary as a snake."

"Angela, is the snake doing anything right now that would be dangerous to you?"

"No."

"Have you ever had a conversation with a snake? "

"No."

"What better time than now? In playing the Love Game, you search for my presence. I AM One with all, including snakes. Open your heart and talk to the snake. Introduce yourself."

Angela faces the serpent. With a tremble in her voice she says, "Hi, I'm Angela. Love asked me to talk to you. I want you to know that I'm afraid of you. I've always been afraid of snakes. Right now, not so much because I'm not alone. Love is with me."

"Hi, I'm Garter Snake. You can call me Gart. I am also afraid of you. Normally, I would slither away as fast as possible, but something is different today. I'm sensing you don't want to hurt me. Plus, no one has ever stopped to talk to me before. My heart is beating much slower now."

"Mine too," says Angela. "Tell me more about yourself, Gart."

"When you came by, I was basking in the warmth of the sun. I don't generate much heat in my body, so I rely on

100

outside temperature. At this time of day, the sunlight peaks through the trees and lands right on this spot. Isn't it amazing that you came at this moment?"

"Yes, it was perfect timing, Gart."

"I like to stay close to the ground. You might say I'm grounded. I move very quietly so I can catch my food as well as keep myself hidden from beings that want to hurt me. I'm one of Love's creatures that helps maintain ecological balance. For example, I help keep pests and insects in control so gardens can grow without using pesticides. I'm another piece of Love's puzzle for life. I learned to be afraid of humans because they would chase my family members down and kill them for no other reason than they themselves were afraid and didn't want me around. I have never done anything to harm people."

"People do crazy things when they are afraid, Gart. They even kill other animals for sport, and sometimes they kill other people. I'm so glad I met you today, and you stopped long enough to talk to me."

"I want you to know one more thing about me, Angela. I transform or rebirth myself a few times a year when I grow new skin and shed my old self. Isn't that what is happening to you right now, Angela? You are expanding your mind and waking up to your Loveself, shedding many of the beliefs that you have had. This magical journey of your life is about to change as you experience a rebirth into Love. Congratulations, Angela."

"I have never touched a snake. May I touch your back? I want the sensation of being connected to you. "

"Yes, Angela. I would like that."

Angela reaches down and gently touches Mr. Snake's back. "Thank you, and have a nice day, Gart."

"I AM here, Angela. Did you see me?

Yes, Love. I see you as Gart."

She smiles and continues down the trail toward the pond. She comes to a grassy clearing. Back in the full sun now. She takes off her shoes and feels the soft grass poking up between her toes. She sees a pond up ahead. Someone is sitting on the bank, dangling his feet in the water.

David senses someone coming up behind him, and he turns to see Angela. He jumps up and says, "Wow! What a wonderful surprise." The two of them hug, and then Angela kisses David on the cheek. David blushes and says, "I like your kiss, Angela."

"Well, I liked it too, DavidLove. Is it OK if I call you DavidLove? What are you doing here?"

"Love woke me up this morning and told me that there was the next level of the Love Game that I could play. If I chose to come to the Peace Pond this morning, I would be given instructions for Level-2. So here I am. How about you, Angela?"

"Love also woke me up and invited me to come here to play Level 2 of the Love Game, too."

"How did you find this place? Have you been here before?"

"No, Love gave me some general instructions to help me fulfill my desire. I used satisfying thoughts, feelings, and intuition to find this spot. I had an incredible experience with a snake on my way here." She then told him about the encounter.

"Angela, Did I tell you that this is the spot where I first saw Love?"

"We didn't get past our encounter with Chickadee before I ran off. I want to apologize. I felt so bad for you because I couldn't tell you what was happening."

"I learned a lot from that experience, Angela, and I really appreciated your Nana talking to me. Are you ready to learn about level 2?"

"Totally, DavidLove. Love, We're ready."

Love responds: "I AM here. In level 1, you encountered beings that were accepting, kind, and friendly, and you were able to see them as me, the Love as they are. The level 2 challenge is to see me in people or beings that you don't like or people or beings that you are afraid of. Angela, you have already started level 2 when you encountered Gart and saw him as Love. For the most part, David, you have been playing the Love Game by yourself. Even though it is not necessary, I invite the two of you to play together on Level 2. That is so you can complement and support each other.

By the end of the day, you will discover how playing the Love Game with someone else at this Level helps you know my presence and see me in challenging situations."

David, before you guys leave, I invite you to introduce Angela to Peace Pond and show her how helpful this Pond can be in playing the Love Game."

"Be happy to, Love. Angela, let's sit down on the edge of the pond and dangle your feet into the water. It's okay if the minnows tickle your toes with their kisses. Now look into the Pond and tell me what you see."

"I see the reflection of you and me sitting next to each other."

"I AM here, Angela and David. You are both seeing me reflected in yourself. I AM you; you are me; we are One."

Angela and David smile, turn to face each other, and say simultaneously, "I see you as Love, and I feel Perfect."

"Please close your eyes and notice how the water relaxes your feet and how the calmness spreads up your legs into your hips. With each breath you take, the calmness continues to rise into your stomach, into your chest, into your neck, and then into your head. Is there anything that is causing you to worry or something you are questioning right now that you want Peace Pond to help you with?"

"Yes. I want to know how I can get my momma back. She left me because she couldn't handle the possibility of me dying of this cancer."

"Let your calmness push any questions or unsatisfying thoughts out the top of your head and watch them sink into the water to be engulfed by Love. Notice how quickly the pond returns to Peaceful silence. You don't have to do anything but to continue to live your life. Love will show you the answer when you least expect it. You don't have to be here at the Peace Pond to have it serve you. You just imagine getting what you want and notice your feelings. Instead of thinking about your mom coming back in the future, create the experience by imagining in detail your mother coming back now. What does she say? What does she smell like? What does her touch feel like? The sensation of being hugged by your mom? If you have unsatisfying thoughts, you can let them go into the pond. If you are feeling tense, imagine dangling your feet in the pond and watching how the tension is replaced with calmness and peace. How are you feeling now?"

"Perfect, DavidLove."

"Let's go and play the Love Game."

Chapter 19

The Challenge of Hate

David and Angela get up and walk back down the path that Angela took to get to the pond. Once they got to the main trail, David asked Angela, "would you like to visit Chickadee?"

"Yes, I left so abruptly the other day; I want to apologize." David took the path toward Chickadee's tree. Up ahead, they saw two boys; one was swinging something over his head. As they got closer, David recognized the boys as Butch and Steve. "I really don't like them, Angela, let's go another way."

Before Angela could answer, Butch calls out, "Hey shrimp, who's your girlfriend?" Butch and Steve run over to them, and Angela gasps when she sees what Butch is swinging over his head. It is Gart. She screams, "Let him go. He won't hurt you." Butch then throws Gart at Angela. Angela catches him, carefully puts him back on the ground, and says, "I'm sorry that this happened to you."

"It is what it is, Angela. Thanks for your kindness." Gart quickly moves off into deeper grass.

Butch turns to David, "What are you doing hanging with a black girl?"

"What black girl are you talking about? I don't see any black girls."

"Are you blind, shrimp," Butch points to Angela.

"She's not black. She is brown, just like all people. We are all shades of brown. Black is like Steve's hair, and she certainly doesn't look like that. As a matter of fact, there are also no white people. Have you ever seen a person as white as a cloud? I can tell you with certainty that her blood is red, just like yours."

"Shrimp, you're not only small, you are an idiot. Don't you know she is a different race?"

"Butch, that's just a story that people have made up to keep us separated. We are all connected. We are One."

"This is stupid talk." Butch turns his attention to Angela and notices her hat. He walks over to her and grabs her hat off.

Steve yells, "She's bald." Both Butch and Steve start laughing.

David jumps between them, trying to get the hat, but Butch holds it too high for him to reach.

Angela says, "It's OK, David. I don't need it." David persists anyway and grabs Butch's arm holding the hat. Butch says, "Don't you ever touch me," punching David in the stomach. David slumps to the ground, trying to catch his breath.

Angela puts her arm around David, "Are you alright?"

Butch then throws Angela's hat up, and it catches on a branch high up in the tree next to them.

David groans. "You're a real jerk, Butch; I hate you. Just leave us alone."

Butch then turns to Steve and says, "What fun would that be?"

Angela then recognizes Butch as the boy who was being berated by his father on Monday when she and her Nana were walking home from the park. She now understands how Butch could be as mean as he was. His Loveself is totally hidden by the abuse he has endured.

"Butch, I see through your tough-guy act. I see you as someone with dreams, maybe of becoming a major league baseball player someday."

"You don't know anything about me, baldy."

"I know that you are no moron, in case anyone has ever said that you were. I know that you want your dad to be kind and love you." Angela looks directly into Butch's eyes. "I see you, Butch." Still looking into Butch's eyes, she reaches her hand up in the air catching her hat as it falls from the tree. She then looks up to see Chickadee sitting on the tree branch where the hat stuck. She smiles and says, "Thanks, Chickadee."

Butch, with his jaw agape, says, "I'm sorry for being mean to you two. Let's go, Steve."

Angela says, "You guys have a nice day."

As they walk off, David asks Angela, "How were you able to keep so cool? I totally went into the survival game."

"For a moment, I defaulted into the survival game when I saw him twirling Gart. The appreciation I felt when I caught Gart and realized he was OK allowed me to return to the Love Game. I didn't have the past experience with being bullied by Butch that you have. I accidentally saw an interaction Butch had with his dad who was verbally and physically abusing Butch, so I felt compassion for him."

"Angela, I guess I really need to practice level 2 of the Love Game. I closed my heart up when he started to bully you. I thought that I had to defend you. I knew my thoughts took me to survival, but I didn't seem to be able to pull myself up by myself. I am sure glad you were here because the Love that you are really lifted me up into that perfect feeling. And it was pure joy seeing the looks on Butch's and Steve's face when you reached up and caught your hat."

David and Angela continued wandering in the park with no destination in mind. They walked past a homeless man who was talking to himself. He was sitting on the ground holding a "Help" sign. He seemed to be very angry at whoever he was talking to. Both David and Angela had been told for years to avoid talking to strangers. They stopped about 20 yards past the man to talk. David says that he has always been afraid of angry people and tries to keep a good distance away.

Angela says, "I feel the same way. What would Love say?"

"Love would probably tell us that we just passed Love by. Angela, I didn't do very well with the Love Game when I was afraid," says David. "This opportunity gives me a second chance."

"Okay, DavidLove. Let's go talk to him."

They walk up to the homeless disheveled man. His head was tilted down. "Excuse me, mister, I'm David, and this is Angela. What is your name?"

The man looks up in surprise to see two young kids. "I'm Roy."

Roy is a veteran who has suffered from Post-Traumatic Stress Disorder and Gulf War Syndrome for 30 years. His weathered look and graying beard make him appear much older than his 55 years.

"I'm sorry, Roy, but we do not have any money to help you. We wonder how you would feel if we just talked with you for a while."

"Yeh, sure."

The two kids sat down on the grass. "How are you doing, Roy?" asks Angela. "We noticed you were talking to someone when we first walked past you. Were you talking with your imagination?"

"Sometimes I get angry with the voices in my head. I was in the war, and sometimes memories of terrible things come back to me. I have a hard time holding down a job because I never know when these voices will take over. Sometimes, the voices are from people who have died. I can't always tell if they are real or not. Are you real?"

Angela responds, "I sure am. Let me touch your hand to prove it."

"Wow. No one that I have been talking to has touched me yet."

Angela touches his hand. He responds with a huge smile and says, "Thank you."

108

David says, "Roy, we too hear voices. My parents are concerned that people will think I am crazy and not treat me very kindly. Has that been your experience?"

"David, people usually just avoid me when they can, and when they can't, they are often unkind. Some will pity me, some will spit on me, some will tell me to get a job, and some will give me a few dollars. Most everyone avoids looking into my eyes. No one before you has stopped to ask how I'm doing. What voices do you hear?"

Angela says, "We talk to Love, what you may call God. Love invited us to play the Love Game, where we look for Love in as many places as we can. To give you an example, let me look into your eyes." Angela looks into Roy's eyes and watches the tears well up. Angela says, "I see the Love that you are, and I feel perfect."

David says, "Let me see, too." David looks into Roy's eyes. "Roy, I see through the wall that you've built around your heart for protection from the memories. I see the real you, the Love that you are, and I also have that Perfect feeling."

"I AM Here."

"Roy, did you hear that?" David asks. "That was Love speaking to us."

"I heard it, but I hear so many things that I don't know whether they were real or not."

Angela says, "Both of us heard it, so it is very unlikely we are all hallucinating the same thing at the same time. The difference between the voices you hear that make you afraid or angry and the voice of Love is the voice of love will tell you everything is fine, perfect, with nothing to fear. When you feel Love's presence, you will have what we call the perfect feeling. This is a combination of happiness, joy, love, appreciation, and peace."

Roy is blown away. "I definitely have a feeling that I can't remember ever feeling before."

They sit there in silence, each basking in the Perfect feeling, when an elderly lady comes up and puts some money into Roy's can. Roy says, "Thank you very much, ma'am."

David looks up and says, "Mrs. Deera, what a wonderful surprise." He jumps up and gives her a hug. "So nice to see you again. This is Roy and Angela. Angela is the girl I told you about. She's the one who led me to you, Mrs. Deera. Angela and I just met Roy and were telling him about the Love Game."

"Nice to meet you, Angela, and you too, Roy. I was on my walk to the park today when I saw you sitting here. What a wonderful surprise."

"Mrs. Deera, how is your back?"

"It hasn't bothered me much since I last saw you on Monday. Without the pain, I AM able to enjoy my walks. So, you two are still playing the Love Game."

Angela says, "Yes, we are. It's been fun."

David says, "After I left you on Monday, I let Love guide me to find God. You gave me a bag of birdseed. Back at the park, I met Chickadee, who suggested I might be more successful in seeing God if I referred to God as Love. After all, they are one and the same. This helped me to finally see Love at the Peace Pond and realize that I had been seeing Love all day. That included seeing you, Mrs. Deera. When I looked into your eyes and experienced the Perfect feeling, I knew I was looking at your true self as Love. Angela and I also saw Roy as Love. He has been going through some tough times, but I know he will be fine. Roy, once your heart opens to your Loveself, you will never forget. You might slip into playing the survival game because that has value, too, but you will return again and again to that Perfect feeling of Love's presence. This will happen often when you listen with your heart and keep your eyes open to possibilities."

Mrs. Deera wishes Roy, "Good luck. I can't stand too long, so I must head home."

"Angela, would you like to walk with Mrs. Deera on her way?"

"Sounds good, DavidLove. Bye, Roy. Hope to see you again."

With beaming eyes, Roy said, "Thank you all for your help and an unforgettable, amazing experience. I think I will play the Love Game with the people that walk by."

"What the hell just happened?" Roy wonders.

"I AM here, Roy."

"You're still here? I thought you would have left with David and Angela."

"I AM always here within your heart. It's time for you to allow yourself to be happy."

"It's too late for me."

"Didn't you feel the perfect feeling of happiness the moment when you first heard me say 'I AM here' with David and Angela?"

"Yes, I guess I did."

"Then how could it be too late for you to create the feeling again? You created happiness when you focused on how appreciative you were to have them stop and talk to you in such an accepting way. At that moment, you didn't think of yourself as broken and unworthy of anything nice. They did not make you happy. That was your own creation when you opened your heart to Me. You said you were willing to play the Love Game with those who pass by. Are you open for an experiment?"

"Yes. I will try anything at this point to feel better."

"Turn your 'Help Me' sign over and draw a heart with the words 'Thank you' under it. Stand up so you can look into the eyes of those who pass and hold the sign for them to see. You are offering thanks for the opportunity to see the Love that they have within their heart. Then, notice your feelings and reactions. You may even choose to wish them a 'loveful' day."

On the walk to her home, Mrs. Deera commented to David and Angela, "You know, David, I would have never even considered stopping to give a homeless person money, let alone talk to one, before I met you on Monday. Your radiant Love is pretty powerful, as is yours, Angela. But together, your combined Love is so brilliant that it would be difficult for anyone to keep their heart sealed around you two."

"Today, Mrs. Deera," David says, "we are playing level 2 of the Love Game. Level one is easier because we look for Love in beings or situations that we like. Level 2 is more challenging because we are looking for Love in beings that we don't like or are afraid of. Initially, we walked past Roy because he was a stranger who was acting a little weird in the way he was talking to himself. I thought this was the perfect opportunity to play the Love Game since I was afraid."

"I AM here."

The trio sings out, "Yes," in perfect harmony. Even as they go their separate ways back home, they still feel connected by Love.

Roy experiments as Love suggested. He notices that the upsetting voices of the demons he had lived with for years quieted. People who would ignore him in the past were now offering him money. One person stops and gives him a donut and a cup of coffee. He saw many more smiles than scowls. He never imagined that meeting two kids and a kind elderly lady could change the way he felt. He decides to take a step toward turning his life around. As dusk approaches, he checks his pockets and finds more money than he has ever received sitting in the park. It was more than enough for a motel room and something to eat.

He walks to the dollar store and buys a toothbrush, toothpaste, a razor, and shaving cream. He then checks in at a motel near the park. He scans his room and notices a clock radio. He flips through the stations until he finds one playing relaxing music. It's been a long time since he has bathed more than what he could do in a gas station bathroom. He takes his clothes off and washes his underwear and socks in the sink, hanging them on the towel rack to dry. He turns the shower on and washes his body and hair. He wonders if the washcloth would be permanently stained with his grime. He is surprised about how much dirt he can hide under his clothes. He rinses out the bathtub and fills it almost full before slipping into the hot water.

He can't stop saying, "Wow, thank you, Love." He reviews his experiences of the day as he enjoys the hot bath and the background music. Initially, there are moments when his thoughts turn to harsh judgments of himself, but these are quickly replaced with appreciation. But even those thoughts dissolve into silence as he relaxes into timelessness.

His awareness returns with an image of being back in his mother's womb, ready to be birthed into a new life. "Yes," he says out loud. "That is just what is happening. There it is again, that perfect feeling I had with Angela, David, and Mrs. Deera. Love, are you here?"

"Yes, Roy. I AM here. You are being birthed into a new life—a life of Love."

After his bath, he stands looking at himself in the mirror, something he has avoided for years. He asks himself, "Do I really deserve the pleasure I am experiencing?"

"Roy, you absolutely deserve pleasure. You deserve the Love that I AM, that you are."

"Thank you, Love." Tears fill Roy's eyes, reflecting the perfect feeling of wonder. "Is it really possible for me to have some meaningful purpose without suffering, given all the bad things I have done in the past?"

"Roy, you have been living your whole life with a valuable purpose, regardless of some of the actions you have taken. Even your presence alone has a purpose. Remember, you are an extension of Love. Do you question that I have a purpose?"

"I don't question that you have a purpose. I just am not sure exactly what it is."

"My purpose is to be. I AM that I AM. I AM the Oneness, I AM Love, I AM is what connects all of existence, I AM the source of creative possibilities."

"How do I fit in?"

"You are a unique and precious piece of the eternal puzzle that is evolving."

He shaves for the first time in a year. He trims his hair with the small scissors in his Swiss army knife and smiles at the new version of himself. He uses the hair dryer in the motel to finish drying his underwear and socks. He pulls out a plastic bag from his backpack. It is a clean T-shirt that he had saved for just the right time. He finishes dressing and heads to the McDonald's down the street. He orders a Big Mac, large fries, and a chocolate milkshake. Roy sits down and slowly eats his meal, savoring each bite to make it last as long as possible. He looks around the room and sees Love in the father and daughter who are sitting together. He sees Love in the construction workers at the corner table laughing. He sees Love in the old man eating by himself. Roy can't help but beam with joy. On his way back to his motel

113

room, he notices one of his homeless friends sitting leaning up on the side of a building. "Hey, Bill, how ya doing?"

"Is that you, Roy? I hardly recognize you without your beard. I'm hanging in there. How about you?"

"I had a really good day," says Roy as he reaches into his pocket. He retrieves the remainder of the money he received that day and hands it to Bill. "I think things are going to pick up for you too. I see the Love that you are, and I feel great."

"Wow, bless you, Roy. I don't want to take all your money. Take some back for tomorrow."

"That's OK, Bill, you keep it. Pass on what you don't need. Tomorrow will take care of itself for me. Bye now."

Roy walks back to his motel with a quirky lightness in his step.

He crawls into bed between the soft, clean sheets, and his last thought as he falls asleep is, "This must be heaven."

Chapter 20

Self -Judgments

Friday, June 14

"Wake up, Roy. I AM here."

Roy was used to being jolted out of his sleep with nightmares. Today was different. He opened his eyes to a wonderful feeling. "Love, is that you?"

"Yes, Roy."

"I can't remember the last time I slept through the night. Is this just another one of my hallucinations?"

"Yes, it is. But instead of the hallucination coming from past experiences stored in your brain and body, this one is coming from your Loveself. I AM your Loveself, and I AM always here. The wonderful, 'perfect,' feeling you are experiencing is available to you, 24/7."

"Why did you wake me up, Love?"

"Roy, I don't usually answer 'why' questions because it takes the fun out of self-discovery, but today I'm going to make an exception. Here is My perfect answer: 'Why not?' However, I do have an invitation for you to meet with David, Angela, and Mrs. Deera at the Peace Pond in the park."

"What time, Love?"

"Do you need to check your calendar?"

"What?"

"That's a joke, Roy. It will be the perfect time. You won't need to look at your watch."

"I didn't know Love makes jokes."

"Sure. Anything I can do to lighten the seriousness of people playing the survival game."

"I'll be there, Love."

Simultaneously, Love awakened David, Angela, and Mrs. Deera with the same invitation as Roy. Each of them also asked Love at what time they should meet. Love replied, "At the Perfect no-time. If you appreciate the moment, you are in now and then step into the next present moment, your intention to meet with the others will guide you to be at the Peace Pond at the Perfect time."

"What do you have planned for today, my Loveself?" asks David.

"I have no plans. My intention today, which is always flexible, is to enjoy playing the Love game with you, Angela, Roy, and Mrs. Deera."

David and Angela arrived on the path to the Peace Pond at the same time and were hugging each other when Mrs. Deera showed up. "I'm glad I saw you when I did," says Mrs. Deera. "I haven't been to the Peace Pond before." Mrs. Deera was carrying a basket, which she placed on the ground so she could hug David and Angela.

"Can I carry your basket?" asks David.

"Yes, thank you. That is very nice of you."

"What's in the basket?" asks Angela.

"Oh, it is a surprise," says Mrs. Deera.

They resume their walk to the Pond.

"I wonder what fun Love has for us today," asks Angela.

"I asked Love and was told there are no plans. Love invites us to play the Love Game together with Roy," says David.

As they approach the pond, they see Roy sitting on the ground next to the edge of the Pond.

Roy sees them coming and stands up to greet them. "Hi, everyone."

"Hi, Roy," the trio responds in unison.

"You've changed since yesterday," says Mrs. Deera.

"Yes, I have. More than I could have imagined and probably more than you could too," says Roy, as he receives hugs from each of them. "You know, I can't remember the last time I had a hug. I was hesitant to let anyone get close to me. I forgot how nice it is."

"I have something for you all," says Mrs. Deera. She opens her basket, and there is a blanket on the top. "Let's spread it out on the ground." Roy takes the blanket, unfolds it, and with a flick of his wrists, the blanket flies up and lands on the ground, all laid out. "I made blueberry muffins, and I have two thermoses. One has hot chocolate for the kids, and the other has coffee for you and me, Roy."

"How wonderful is this," says Angela. Mrs. Deera invites them to sit down on the blanket while she pours the drinks into individual cups.

"Thank you so much, Mrs. Deera," Roy says.

"You're welcome, Roy, but please call me Amma."

The four of them were quiet as they ate the muffins and sipped their drinks.

Roy breaks the silence. "I have been in heaven since meeting you all yesterday. I can't express my gratitude enough for the Love and kindness you have shown me. I AM ready to follow my Loveself into new adventures."

"I AM here, everyone."

"We are too," responds Mrs. Deera.

"I invite you to continue playing level 2 of the Love Game, but today, I suggest you focus your attention on yourself instead of others."

"I thought that in level 2, the focus for finding Love was directed to those we fear or dislike," says David.

"Exactly," says Love. "But that also includes yourself. You all have had times where you really didn't like yourself. yes? Times when you bullied yourself with unkind labels. Do any of you really like yourself just as you are? How many of you can Love yourself while standing stark naked in front of a crowd of people who are laughing and pointing fingers at you? How many of you can still keep your heart open to your Loveself when someone is yelling at you for making a mistake? Explore with each other those unlikeable aspects. It may have been the mistakes you've made, maybe something you regret or feel guilty about, or shame about some aspect of your body or mind. Ready for some fun?"

David speaks first. "I don't like my body. I don't like my small size and that I'm not very good at baseball or football. I don't like myself when people make fun of me, criticize me, or push me around. I feel really bad when I make a mistake in school because I want others to see me as smart. I lie sometimes to avoid punishment for something I did wrong, but then I feel bad about lying. Sometimes I feel guilty when I have thoughts that I want to really hurt Butch for bullying me. He makes me so mad, and I feel powerless to do anything about it. I just can't see myself as Love or Perfect when I think of any of these things."

"Thanks," says Mrs. Deera. "Before finding the perfection in your judgments and feelings, David, how about we all share what we don't like about ourselves? Angela, would you like to go next?"

"Okay, Mrs. Deera," Angela says. "For me, I don't feel very pretty. I don't like that I have cancer. I wonder if I am being punished for being bad. I hate that I'm bald. I don't like the darkness of my skin, either. I don't like that I am ashamed of my naked body and must hide it from others, especially now that my breasts are starting to grow. I am even embarrassed when I am examined by doctors and nurses. Nana tells me that I have to wear something so no one can see the bulge of my nipples. I try to avoid being the center of attention out of embarrassment. I can't stop thinking that it is my fault that my momma left me."

"I appreciate your honesty, Angela. How about you, Roy?" asks Amma.

"The things I don't like about myself could fill a landfill," says Roy. "My war started early in life. It seems I have been fighting someone, but mostly myself, my whole life. Life at home was tough, and I was a bully at school. I was frequently

118

in trouble for fighting. I didn't know any other way to deal with the intensity of the anger I was experiencing. I was arrested for putting a guy in the hospital. The fight was over something really stupid, but I couldn't control my rage. The judge gave me a choice: jail time or the Marines. Joining the Marines seemed to be an acceptable way to act out my anger. I convinced myself that I could be of value in protecting the people of Yemen by killing Iraqi aggressors. If I hadn't joined the Marines, I might've killed someone here and ended up in jail or worse. But now, I constantly beat myself up for joining the Marines and losing control of my mind. If I hadn't joined, I wouldn't have been in the Gulf War and killed hundreds of people, many of whom were innocent civilians. I wouldn't have seen my buddies blown into pieces by landmines. I have lived with the Gulf War Syndrome of constant body pain, memory loss, fatigue, and sometimes diarrhea for 30 years. No one has yet found a remedy for this sickness. Many doctors denied that this syndrome really exists. Recently, however, researchers have related it to being exposed to Sarin Gas, and the symptoms are made worse when you have PTSD. The voices in my head, my anxiety, and frequent outbursts of anger paralyzed me.

The children and Mrs. Deer listen spellbound and feel sadness at Roy's recollections.

"I alienated my family and lost friends. Up until yesterday, I was living alone in the hell that I deserved as punishment for all those bad things that I had done. There were times when I tried to kill myself. Each time, something stopped me. I still don't understand how meeting you guys yesterday got me to come out of my darkness. Even though I feel more accepting of myself today, I can't erase the past, and I can't imagine seeing it as perfect."

David, tears flooding his eyes, rubs his stomach and says, "Wow, I don't know why, but my stomach started to ache while listening to you, Roy."

Angela squeezes David's hand and whispers to him, "I AM here." "You have touched me deeply, too, Roy."

"Thank you, Roy, for allowing us into your heart," says Amma. "What you have experienced is so foreign to anything that I have experienced myself. Seeing war pictures on the news doesn't begin to touch the impact of actually being there. I forget that even when the external wars end, inner wars don't and can be devastating."

Amma goes on to say, "Now that I am 80, and most of my life is over, the regrets have piled up. At times, I still think that if I had been a better mother to Maggie, she wouldn't have killed herself. I hate that I am old and don't have the energy to do the things I could have when I was younger. My value came from caring for others. My purpose was to be a supportive wife, a good mother, grandmother, and friend. I lost that purpose when my son left home, and my husband and best friend died. Now, I'm not even sure I was a good mom because my son doesn't visit with me very often. I felt lonely and depressed before meeting David earlier this week. I used to go to church just to have some social contact but haven't felt motivated to do so lately. I get angry with myself on days that I sit around and watch TV. I could go on and on, but I will stop here."

"Thanks, Amma," says Roy.

"Mrs. Deera, I really appreciate that you, too, have experienced body shame," says Angela. "What now, Love? How do we find Love in these regrets, shame, and guilt each of us is feeling?"

"I AM here. When you have allowed your heart to open to your Loveself, it is easy to experience that Perfect feeling. But what happens when you become aware that you are in the midst of the survival game, berating yourself or making choices that are unkind to your well-being? How do you shift into the Love Game when you are telling yourself that you were stupid for making a mistake? How about when you are deep into your story of loneliness or suffering? What might you do when you are throwing negative labels at yourself?"

The four of them wait in wonder for Love's answer.

"I have gifted you with the power to create your own experiences, which you have in the form of shame, guilt, and regret using self-judgments. This same power of imagination gives you the ability to create the perfect feeling associated with Love and happiness. It is up to you to decide how you want to use your creativity. You are never alone. If you feel stuck, ask for help. Talk to me. The silence of Peace

Pond can assist you in shifting from your survival game perspective of self-condemnation to one of Love by seeing yourself as I see you: perfect and not flawed nor broken. Let your imagination immerse your self-judgments into the Peace of the silent deep water and notice how the feeling of My presence opens your heart to them."

"Love, are you saying that you see wars and killing people as perfect?" asks Roy.

"Of course, I do, Roy. If it happens, it is perfect. It is a perfect outcome reflecting how some people are choosing to play the survival game."

"Let's talk about self-care. Everyone, in every moment, cares for themself in some way—sometimes in ways that seem unhealthy to themselves or others, and sometimes in kind, nurturing ways. You may care for your physical, emotional, or spiritual well-being. You can care for yourself with an open heart or not. The way you care for yourself will influence the reality of your experiences. The opportunity to create experiences is what you signed up for when your spirit incarnated itself into your body."

"Love, how does judging myself as old and unattractive be a way for me to care for myself?" asks Amma. "I can't see the benefit."

"This answer goes for Amma as well as the rest of you. There is always a self-care benefit to every thought, belief, and action. I invite you to connect with the silence of Peace Pond and let the insights rise to the surface. Share your discoveries with each other."

The group falls into silence as they look at the stillness of the Pond. Each person offers to the Pond the question that is foremost on their mind. They watch as their questions disappear and then their thoughts. Their eyes close as they open their hearts to receive.

The perfect amount of time passes, and one by one, their closed eyes smile.

Chapter 21

Unwanted Feelings

"I AM here, Love Ones. Roy, how about sharing your experience first?"

"I asked pond if I can be forgiven for what I've done so I can find some peace. Initially, my thoughts went to reliving the moments in my life when I lost control of my anger. I justified my actions by blaming others. All those memories dropped into the pond. I noticed as I continued looking into the pond that fewer and fewer thoughts were arising, and when they did arise, I didn't have the physical reaction I would normally experience. I don't know whether I fell asleep or not because I don't remember any thoughts coming. When I regained awareness, I was floating above the Pond, watching myself and others sitting on its edge. Then came that perfect feeling that I had when I looked into Angela and David's eyes. From the depth of the pond came the answer I had asked for."

"I got the message that forgiveness implies letting go of judgments. Love doesn't need to forgive me because it is not the nature of Love to judge. Judgments are man-made, not Love-made. I don't need to fight my judgments or anger to make them go away. I can accept them the moment they arise and know they come from playing the survival game. When playing the survival game, forgiveness is a way to move past blaming myself or others for the pain that I have experienced in the past and still hold on to. Alternatively, I could choose to shift to playing the Love Game in the present moment, as we are doing now. When I view the perfection of my life from my LoveSelf, I don't need to forgive anything or anyone, including myself."

His companions nod and smile.

"I also asked Pond how my anger and guilt was a way to care for myself. Peace tells me my anger is a way to show me that I'm not getting what I want. If I stay focused on what I don't have, the anger builds up. Sometimes, acting out the anger, even hurting others, gives me temporary emotional relief and the feeling of power that I lack. Then, the guilt comes to remind me that I'm focused on the past and fighting it in the present moment. I was so afraid of how destructive my anger had been in the past; keeping the guilt made me turn the anger to myself instead of other people. The guilt was one thing that kept me alone, avoiding relationships and hurting people. I noticed I was guilt-free when immersed in the Peace Pond. I realized that if I could be guilt-free for one moment, I could be free for more and more moments. I could take charge of my life and stop fighting. I could choose to tell a different story and allow my LoveSelf to create new present moments. Ones that don't label me a victim or a villain, eases my anger, and celebrates life. I am aware now that everything I have experienced has brought me to this Perfect Feeling in this Perfect moment. I wasn't ready to open my heart before meeting Angela and David. I am so grateful and hope that I can be an inspiration to others as they are to me."

"Roy, Love, welcome Home. Who would like to go next?" asks Love.

"I would," Angela says. "I asked how feeling ashamed of who I am was a way to care for myself. I was taught that in order for a young black girl to be safe in this world, I needed to keep a low profile, not stand out or be the center of attention. Being the best or the worst, pretty or ugly, smart or dumb, too skinny or too fat could set me up as a target for bullying. I tried to fit in by being mediocre. Some things were out of my control, such as skin shade or hair texture. My baldness certainly set me apart. My shame kept me quiet and shy. I even hid my art from others to avoid their judgments. I am glad that I protected my art because it gave me time to develop my creativity without the 'shoulds and shouldn'ts' of others.

Angela reflects: "Pond told me that shame is looking at myself through the eyes of others who are playing the survival game. My self-worth depended on the opinions of others. However, even if I hustle for complements, and get them, I can't embrace them. I don't value myself.

My ego's survival mindset is always eager to offer a story that confirms my beliefs of unworthiness. I have tried to be what others want me to be by sidestepping their negative judgments. I was putting more attention and importance on being accepted by others than I was being authentic to my LoveSelf. I knew that the feeling of shame was not what I wanted; instead, I wanted self-acceptance and Love. Pond also said that experiencing shame helps me develop empathy and compassion for others. It reminds me that I can continue judging others with my conditioned survival mind or choose to see them through the eyes of Love."

"Wow, that's awesome, Angela," says David.

"I'm so proud of you," Mrs. Deera chimed in.

Angela continues, "Pond told me that it was no accident that I was born black, had an alcoholic mother and no father to help raise me. And it had absolutely nothing to do with my value as a Love soul. Plus, it is also no accident that I have cancer, found David, and now see and hear God as Love. Everything has a perfect Purpose. Being here is my precious opportunity to learn about my LoveSelf, create experiences, and see how I affect others when I see the Love they are through my open heart."

"Thanks, Angela," says Roy. "So much of what came from your experience with Pond also applies to me."

"Me too," says David. "Can I go next, Mrs. Deera?"

"Please do, David."

"Before this week, I have been afraid of people. I asked Peace Pond how fear of people benefits me. It can happen unexpectedly, but I am always on guard for being hurt. The hurt may come physically from verbal attacks, rejection, or abandonment. I fear them all. Other than my parents, who I can't avoid, I try to keep a safe distance from others, expecting them to reject me. I often reject them first before they will do it to me. I think that if I was good enough, it would be easier for people to accept me. That's probably why I also have a fear of making mistakes. I am not as hard on myself if I make a mistake and no one else knows about it. But if someone else knows, I start with shame; then I beat myself for not knowing better. To avoid those feelings, I would sometimes get into arguments to prove I was right. No matter whether I was right or not, getting into an argument felt bad. How can making mistakes be perfect when I feel anything but perfect?"

"I hear you," said Roy.

"I didn't need to say anything more. I imagined slowly walking into the pond, feeling the deep sense of peace rise up in me until I was fully immersed. I imagined myself playing like a dolphin with the others in a pod, swimming deep, then springing up in the air. My thoughts about fear and people disappeared as I focused on the pure joy of being me. I got out of the water and sat at the edge, drying off, appreciating the warm sun and the stillness around me. I forgot that I had asked the pond any questions. Then, from my heart, I heard Love speak."

"David, your fear of people has been an important factor in the fine-tuning of your ability to sense their emotions. This has served you by knowing when to get close and when to back away. It has allowed you to avoid the pain of rejection. This was perfect then, but as you now have seen the light of your Loveself, your need to rely on others for your self-worth will dissipate, along with your fear. Your ability to empathize and act with compassion will allow you to be of service to everyone's benefit."

"What about my fear of mistakes, Love? Will they go away too?"

126

"No, the fear of mistakes won't go away. Anytime you find yourself playing the survival game, mistakes will happen. In the survival game, a mistake is simply a man-made label for not getting the desired outcome. Attaching a negative judgment, such as bad or stupid, to a mistake leads to undesired feelings. Mistakes have value in giving you information about the focus of your attention and how you want to proceed from that point. When you allow yourself to see life as I do, there are no mistakes. Nothing is imperfect. Perfection, like Love, is what it is. What you can appreciate is that you now have the choice to see life like I do."

"Thank you, David," says Mrs. Deera. "Hearing your story, as well as Roy's and Angela's, reminds me that we are not so different in experiencing shame, guilt, and fear. I asked Peace Pond about the benefit of feeling depressed and lonely."

"Before this week, I was grieving the loss of companionship, physical abilities, and my purpose for living. I don't want to die, but I don't want to continue living without a purpose, either. I feel I am running out of time to find one, too. I asked the pond to help me clarify my purpose for living. I also was curious to know how feeling bad would help me feel good."

"I imagined myself floating serenely on the pond. The water tenderly massaged me, easing every breath into a rhythm of peace. Tension dissolved into the warm embrace of the quiet waters. My mind wandered into the tranquil realm of unity, where separation ceased to exist. There was no time, only now."

Love answers. "The only reason to hold on to any thought or feeling is because you believe it has value. You may not always recognize the benefit of an unwanted feeling, especially in the role of self-care. In the survival game, unwanted feelings are sometimes held tight to preserve and care for a belief. Your long-standing story is that getting old is bad, that you will be a burden, that wrinkles are unattractive, or that you have to do something to be of value. Those stories create your experience. Your conditioned survival mind is vested in maintaining the beliefs, and these beliefs are nothing more than the habitual stories you tell yourself. In a sense, you have become addicted to the stories. Addictions are a challenge to overcome in the survival game but can be easier by playing the Love Game. As we have spoken before, change the story, and you will create a different reality. You don't need to know specifically what your purpose is in order to accept that your presence has great value in every moment. For example, your purpose at this moment is to float on the Peace Pond and to witness your life through the eyes of Love. The universal effects of that one thing have awesome eternal benefits. Each moment has its own perfect purpose."

"Mercy, that's good to hear," Mrs. Deera exclaimed.

"Any feeling has the benefit of reflecting the story you are telling. If you are having an unsatisfying feeling, you have the choice to change your story, change your focus, or change the game you are playing. Before this week, you had been telling the story of loneliness and depression. Now, you have experienced firsthand how playing a different game has uplifted you and opened up so many possibilities that come when seeing life through the eyes of Love. Your loneliness and depression have led you here but are no longer needed from this point on. Rejoice!

The group remained in stunned silence as they let the messages received penetrate. Words seemed useless. Then, each one stood up, looked into each other's eyes, crossed their hands over their hearts, and then opened them with palms up to the person they faced, inviting a heart-to-heart hug. Everyone except Roy then headed home. Roy felt the pond was his home.

Walking from the pond gave David time to reflect on his morning experience, as well as the experiences of the others. There were aspects of all their stories that applied to him. No matter what the person looks or acts like on the surface, we seem to be challenged with similar issues. He concluded that it was hard to like himself when he played the survival game. He was always comparing himself to others. But in this moment, his heart was opened wide, seeing beauty everywhere. He was happy to be alive. When he got home, his dad was working in the garden.

"Hey, Dad, how's it going?"

"To tell you the truth, David, I'm a little stressed. Working in the garden, connecting with nature, helps calm me."

"Can I help?" David asks.

"With the stress or the garden?" Dad asks.

"I can offer you the presence of my Loveself while we work together to nurture ourselves and the garden, too."

"Maybe this is a good time, David, to tell you about what 'I love you' means to me and why I find it hard to express it in words."

They sit down at the patio table, and Dad continues his story. "My dad and mom never showed affection for each other in front of others. I didn't hear them use the word 'love.' I once asked my dad why he didn't say the words, and he responded that he didn't need to. He said he didn't trust the words, only how people behaved toward him and he toward others. He said people try to manipulate others with the word 'love' in order to get something in return. My dad said it was more important to express his care for others by his actions. I don't remember him yelling or exhibiting strong emotions, either positive or negative. One time, when I was crying about something I wanted and couldn't have, he calmly told me it was very important to always control your emotions. It's OK for women to cry, but boys and men need to keep their anger and distress private. It is selfish to subject others to your feelings as if they are responsible for them."

Dad went on. "He worked a lot and didn't spend much time with me. I overheard my mother asking Dad to spend more time at home. He responded with, 'My job is to support my family by keeping a roof over our heads and food on the table. Once I feel I have done that adequately, I will consider spending more time at home. He was, however, strict about not working on Sundays and always going to church. That was the day I spent the most time around him. After church, I would go out to the garden with him. Often, we would work together for hours without saying one word to each other. I was twelve when my dad died suddenly. He had some kind of heart problem. I did my best to control my tears because that's what I thought he would want me to do.

I had to be strong for my mom. My mom had to get a job, so I was alone a lot, just like you were after your mom divorced your father. She never remarried and didn't talk about Dad very often. My older brother left home not long after my dad died, so I didn't have much of a male role model going into my teenage years. I realize now how many of my father's perspectives about expressing emotions have stuck with me. I am still uncomfortable saying the words 'I love you.'"

"David, from the moment I first met you, you touched my heart. The way you showed your excitement at seeing me when your mom and I were dating was so endearing. The way you hugged me left me feeling joy in a way that I had never experienced before. I wanted to be a part of your life as much as I wanted to be a part of your mother's life. I care so deeply for your well-being. I never want you to fear that I will hurt you. I never want you to fear that I will intentionally leave you. I may die, but I will not abandon you. Yes, I have been afraid since you have been talking to and seeing God or Love. It is so outside my experience and anyone I know that I worry about you enduring the pain of ridicule or rejection. I have relied on my faith in Jesus to get me through troubling times, and I want you to know Jesus, too."

"Dad, I know Jesus as Love as I know you. I don't need to look to a historical figure to know Love."

David looks at his dad and says, "I look through your eyes straight into your heart and see the Love that you are, and I feel perfect. I don't need you to tell me that you love me. I see your presence as Love."

David sees tears welling up in his dad's eyes for the very first time. David crosses his hands over his heart and then extends his palms up toward his father, just as he did with Angela, Roy, and Mrs. Deera. Dad accepts the invitation and joins David in a timeless hug, during which he hears the words, "I AM here." Dad shakes his head with a furrowed brow, quickly passes it off as nothing, and then refocuses on the hug.

130

Chapter 22

The Uncontrollable

Saturday, June 15

"Wake up, Angela and David. I AM here."

"Ok, Love, I AM awake."

"Me too," says David.

"Angela, I invite you to go over to David's house this morning. I Am going to introduce you to Love Game Level 3."

"Sounds interesting. Usually, we go to the Pond," says Angela. "I'm curious about the change."

"Isn't being curious exciting, Angela? A new place, a new time, a new adventure embracing uncertainty. Life is full of wonderful possibilities."

"I'm excited to learn about another Level of the Love Game," says David. Angela, we can get something to eat at my house before we start the Game.

David goes down to the kitchen and tells his mom that Angela is coming over to play and asks if she can eat breakfast here?"

"Of course, David. What are you two going to do today?"

"I'm uncertain what will happen. Love is going to introduce us to Level 3 of the Love Game."

"Sounds interesting. David, you told me about Level I but I don't remember you saying anything about Level 2."

"I didn't? Sorry, mom. Level 2 was finding Love in beings that we don't like or are afraid of. That was a challenge for me especially when facing Butch. Angela did better at Level 2. She found Love in Butch despite being bullied by him. She has always been afraid of snakes and after having a conversation with one, she was able to touch it. We both found Love in an angry homeless veteran named Roy."

"I'm not sure I Am comfortable with you interacting with homeless men, David."

"It's fine mom, Mrs. Deera was also there. The Love we experienced together changed Roy's life."

Angela rings the doorbell and David rushes to answer. "Hi, DavidLove."

"I'm so glad you came, Angela. Come on in."

Mom comes out of the kitchen finding the kids hugging each other. David says, "Mom, this is my good friend Angela I have been telling you about. Angela, this is my mom."

"Nice to finally meet you, Angela. Come on, sit down and I'll get you something to eat. We have some orange juice, sweet rolls, and cereal. Does that interest you? I can cut up a banana for your cereal if you like.

"Thank you, Mrs. Walden. Cereal with bananas sounds good.

David pulls up a chair for Angela next to him. "This is my brother Tom, who is almost finished eating. My older brother Michael is upstairs still asleep.

"After we finish breakfast Angela, I would like to show you my favorite place to go in the woods behind my house."

"Is that where you met Deer?"

"Yes, it is. Maybe she will be by today so I can introduce you to her."

I would like that very much, DavidLove."

Mom sits down with a cup of coffee and says, "Angela, "I understand you have cancer. How is it going for you?"

"Not too good, the chemotherapy makes me very tired and of course, there is the baldness. I am still hopeful that I will get better."

"I hope you get better too. I see that you have brought a drawing pad. Are you an artist?

"I am. I use my drawings as a journal of my life instead of writing words.

David's Dad enters the room and asks, "Who do we have here?"

"This is my friend Angela, Dad."

"Well, how do you do, Angela? David has told me about some of your experiences together. It's nice to finally meet you."

"It's nice to meet you too, Mr. Walden.

"You two enjoy your day. I'm going out to mow the lawn.

David and Angela finish their breakfast and David asks his mom for a carrot just in case he and Angela see the deer.

Mom says, "be careful."

David and Angela go out the back door. David grabs two seat cushions on the patio chairs and then leads the way into the woods.

"Where are the paths, David," asks Angela.

"There are none. I go a different way each time to avoid creating paths. That way it makes it harder for others to find my secret hiding spaces."

"I've never been in the woods like this before. Do you worry about getting lost?"

"I never think about getting lost. I always find my way back." It wasn't more than a 10-minute walk when David said, "this is the tree I was sitting in when you drew the picture." He put the cushions on the ground and invited Angela to sit down."

Angela looks at the tree and asks, "how did you get to the first limb? It's too high to reach."

"Do you see that smaller tree? It has lower limbs so I climb up on that tree until the limbs intersect with the larger tree then I cross over."

"That's impressive David. What should we talk about?"

"You said something yesterday that interested me. You said you were ashamed of your naked body and must hide it from others especially now when your breasts are starting to grow. Do you wish you could be comfortable being naked with me?"

"I think I would like for you to see me naked. I feel you would accept me just as I am. I would also like to see you naked, DavidLove. Would you like to take off your clothes with me?"

"I don't know why my heart suddenly started beating very fast and I'm feeling butterflies, " says David. "Yes, I would really like to be naked together."

"I feel the butterflies too, DavidLove.

David stands up and pulls his shorts and underwear down then takes off his t-shirt. Angela looks at him for a moment and takes her clothes off including her hat exposing her baldness.

Angela says, "I feel so comfortable with you and not embarrassed at all. I want our whole bodies touching", as she puts her arms around David's shoulders pulling him close. Their breathing becomes synchronized in silence. Minutes passed in seconds. They break enough to look into each other's eyes. David says it first, "I see the Love that you are and I feel Perfect."

Angela then responds the same. "I have never felt so fully accepted by another person my whole life. I see the Love that you are and I feel Perfect too."

The sound of footsteps interrupts this special moment. David and Angela react by hugging each other tighter. A brief thought raced through their minds that people wouldn't understand and they would get in trouble for being naked. This feeling was followed by a surge of relief when a deer appeared. Their bodies relaxed. The deer came close for each of them to look the deer straight into her eyes and then pet it. To their surprise, she lay down on the ground before them. The kids got dressed and sat down on their cushions facing the deer. Angela reaches over to hold David's hand.

"I AM Deer. I AM here.

"Hi, Deer. It's great to see you again", says David. This is my special good friend Angela."

David reaches into his pocket to retrieve the carrot. He breaks it in half and gives Angela one piece. He then offers his piece to the deer. The deer leans its head forward to get the carrot. In a few chews, it's gone. Angela follows by offering the deer her carrot.

Deer says, "thank you for the carrot. I AM here as Love to introduce you to Level 3 of the Love Game. Ready?"

David says, "before we start, let's address the elephant in the woods. From your perspective, Love, how did you view Angela and my nakedness together?"

"David, you realize that as a deer, I run around naked and wild. I poop in the open and I don't care who sees me having sex. To answer your question, I saw two love-selves freely connecting with each other to co-create a perfect Love experience. You have been given a body to enjoy, not to be ashamed of. I realize those playing the survival game have placed all kinds of rules and restrictions on the freedom you were experiencing. Using discretion about the timing and privacy of your actions may serve you by avoiding the consequences that survival game players are all too ready to impose on you. Anything else?"

The kids shake their heads.

"The intention of level 3 is to find Love in unwanted situations or unsatisfying thoughts or feelings. Unwanted situations are often where you have no control. These situations can be the result of some acts of nature, weather, accidents, wars, illness, injustice, crime, or prejudice. It may include society standards, government laws, school rules, and expectations from parents or caregivers. It may also be when your teacher springs a pop quiz on you. You get the picture. From your ego's point of view, one of the most uncontrollable situations is what actually happens to you after you die."

"Angela, one obvious uncontrollable situation that you have been experiencing recently is cancer. Can you tell David about your experiences with cancer and the prospect of dying?"

"Before last week it would have been really hard for me to think about Love and cancer at the same time. Cancer really sucks. Just hearing the diagnosis sent me into a panic.

Before that, I never thought about dying. I heard all kinds of stories about cancer and advice about what I should or shouldn't do came from every corner. Some people couldn't keep horror stories to themself. I was told to pray and if I prayed hard enough and was good enough maybe a miracle would happen. I was told that my illness was in God's hands and he would decide whether I would get better or not. This made me angry. I didn't want to be a puppet. Some people judged me, assuming that I must have done something wrong or bad to merit getting cancer.

Angela paused to breathe and let that thought sink in. "And of course, I was asking myself the same question. There were people in the hospital including the staff that had a hard time looking me in the eyes. My Momma couldn't either. She was more comfortable being in a bar than being around me at least before she disappeared. No one really wanted to talk to me about dying or what would happen at the end, and what would happen after."

Angel continued: The chemotherapy zapped my energy, made me vomit, have a sore butt from the diarrhea and lose my hair. There was pain from getting IVs, blood tests, shots, belly cramps, and headaches. I worry about the pain getting worse before I die and how I was going to handle it. I worry about how sad my Nana would be when I passed. The only friends I have were kids I met in the hospital and those friendships tended to be brief. I was depressed that I might never have the chance to fall in love, get married, and have children. I was sad that I would never have the time to become a successful artist."

"Now, I think about you DavidLove, and what we have experienced together. I wonder if I would have ever found the Love that I am if I hadn't had cancer. I now know that God exists as Love in each of us and this Loveself, when allowed to shine, can have a healing effect on ourselves as well as others. Healing doesn't mean that my cancer will necessarily go away. It does mean that I can choose to accept the moment as it is and live happily with my heart open to Love. I could also choose to resist being happy by allowing fear to take me out of the present. I really dislike feeling afraid and know that I can ease my distress by surrendering it to my Loveself.

"What do you mean by surrender?" asks David.

"It means I am willing to give up the fight to control situations and others. I accept my feelings and thoughts. I then can shift to seeing what is before me in the moment through the eyes of Love."

"Angela, does accepting the moment and the cancer you have mean that you don't want to get treatment," David asks.

"No, David. I still have a desire to feel better and to return to my healthy physical self. I still have dreams about the future. I can take an action that will help me, such as chemotherapy. I now know how to create the effect feeling of Love's presence. I see the value of cancer as a guide to point me toward what is really important in my life above just surviving.

"Thank you, Angela for sharing your experiences," says Deer. "David, what have been your experiences with uncontrollable situations?"

"The time I fell out of the tree was uncontrollable. But the interesting thing about that was it happened so fast, and the fall probably lasted less than 10 seconds from the top of the tree, I had no fear. I didn't have any time to think except to notice when I was hitting branches on the way down. I never thought that I could die until after I landed, got up, and saw all the things that could have killed me if I hadn't landed in the perfect place.

But really the most distressing uncontrollable situation is the one we have been speaking about. "I don't want Angela to die and I can't do anything about it. I don't want to lose her. When I think about that, I lose control of my thoughts and sink into playing the survival game imagining all kinds of terrible feelings. I get upset with myself because I know that I will feel better if I only see the situation through Love's eyes but the fearful voices speak louder. Running away as I have done in the past, doesn't feel right for me now. I don't want to leave her."

"DavidLove, are you happy in this moment with Deer, Love, and me," asks Angela"

"Yes. All I have to do is look into your eyes to feel perfect."

"So even in the midst of talking about Angela dying, you were still able to be happy, " says Deer.

Angela's Love will always be here even when her body isn't. I AM here and always will be," says Love. The memory of your perfect feeling experiences will lead you back to your Loveself even when the survival game voices start screaming judgments and fears.

Thank your moments of distress for reminding you to focus your attention on creating the perfect feeling. If your thoughts get too upsetting for you, you can always give them a bath in the Peace Pond. David, there is nothing your Loveself can't handle."

"Okay you two, I am going to reveal a secret to a question that humans have posed for thousands of years and most have struggled with finding an answer. The question they ask is "why am I here?" Since I don't answer "why" questions, I am rephrasing it to "what is my purpose for living?"

David and Angela looked alert in anticipation of the answer.

"Simply, your purpose for living is to create a Love story. It's not about doing anything specific. It's about the fun of creating experiences and physical manifestations through your choices of thoughts, stories, perspectives, and actions. As you two are creating your individual life's love story, you are also co-creating one together as well as with everyone you come in contact with. You create the reality of a love story when you see your life's experiences through the eyes of Love."

David asks, "Does that mean that a person can fail at life if they don't create a Love story?"

"You can't fail because each life you live is offering you experiences that will ultimately paint a picture of your love story. Life can be just like the love stories you see in movies. It may start rocky with lots of ups and downs but in the end, everything works out. I want you to know that everyone no matter what their life is like now, will in the end live happily ever after. When this body you are living in dies, it does not end your story. Your soul will have choices about how it wants to continue. Some souls choose to merge totally into the Love I AM. Others choose to continue writing their love story while in spirit form as they support individuals who are still living in their physical bodies. Some souls return to another body. All Love stories flow into me as I AM."

"What will happen to me when I die? What will I choose," asks Angela.

David raises his voice and blurts out, "You're not gonna die!"

"I will die someday. It would be nice if the cancer would go away. If it doesn't, I will surrender to Love. I don't feel like fighting cancer."

"Ok, I get it. I'll come back to the present," David says.

Deer says, "Angela, you said that you will die someday. Do you know that someday never comes? There is only now and you will only know the moment you die and not before. You will know what you choose will happen only after your body dies. Nothing is predestined."

"What if others don't like the Love story we create," David asks. "I think some people, like Butch, think that Angela and I shouldn't be friends together because we don't have the same skin color. I expect that my mom might think we're too young to be hugging and kissing each other?"

"Your Loveself isn't interested in the stories others tell about you. It's only interested in the story you tell yourself. Be true to yourself beyond seeking approval from others."

"You can appreciate your past, including your pain and suffering to the extent that it has served its purpose by leading you here. But here in this moment the past ends. 'Now' is what matters. You both have taken a step up from relying on the survival game to find Love. Now you have a choice that you were unaware of before. You can play the Love Game and see Love everywhere. Just by allowing your Loveself to shine, you contribute to a major shift in the consciousness of the universe."

Angela turns to David. "I AM so grateful that we are here together. I like the way our Loveselves reflect off each other creating the perfect feeling. Now that I know this feeling, I can use it as a compass to refocus my direction anytime I move away from Love into fear. I enjoy how we can be naked with each other, not just physically, but how our naked hearts have merged."

David can't hold back his tears of joy. He holds Angela's face in his hands, looks into her eyes, gently kisses her lips, then wraps his arms around her putting his head on her chest to hear her heartbeat. "I feel perfect, Angela Love."

"My DavidLove, my sweet Love, I AM here," Angela says with beaming eyes.

I AM here. Deer stands up and nuzzles against the kids. "It's time for me to walk a bit. See you two Love birds later."

David and Angela hold hands as they walk back to the house.

Chapter 23

Another Wake-up Call

Sunday, June 16

"Wake up David. Please wake up."

"Ok, Love". David opened his eyes to see his mom bending over him. "Oh, it's you, Mom, What's up?"

His mother with tears running down her cheeks, kisses and hugs him. David then realizes he isn't in his own bed. "Where am I, Mom?"

"Nurse, come quick," his mom calls out. "You are in a hospital, honey. You've been real sick. I am so happy that you are awake. I love you so much."

David looks around to see monitors and a tube coming from his arm and going to a bag of water hanging on a pole. He hears a beeping sound from the monitor. His mouth is dry.

A nurse runs into the room to see David trying to sit up in bed. "Lie back down, David, so I can check you."

Mom picks up the phone and calls David's father who was getting some coffee at the hospital cafe. "David's awake! Yes, he seems Okay. The nurse is checking him now."

"I'm Nurse Lenus. How are you feeling David?"

"Like I just woke up. What happened? Why am I here?"

I'll answer all your questions but first I want to make sure you are all right. Okay?

"Do you know where you are?"

"Mom said I was in the hospital."

"What is the last thing you remember?"

"I was going to bed. I remember being really tired."

Do you know what day it is now?"

It is Sunday. I was just with Angela yesterday playing in the woods behind our house. We had a great talk with Love.

Mom tells nurse Lenus, "I don't know who Angela is and of course, he was here yesterday. What's happening?"

"What are you talking about Mom? I've been seeing Angela for the last week. I told you that we were playing a game with God, you know, Love."

Mom starts crying and shakes her head. The nurse tries to reassure her saying, "It's okay, it is too soon to tell about his recovery. Let me continue with the evaluation."

Turning to David, she says, "David, I'm going to hold up my finger, without turning your head, follow the movement of my finger with your eyes. That was fine. Open your mouth. Now you can close it. Can you squeeze my fingers?"

David squeezes the nurse's hands. "That's really good, you are strong. Can you move your feet now?" David moves both his feet. "Great. You seem to be doing exceptionally well, young man." She turns to David's Mom and says, "your doctor has been called and she will do a more extensive evaluation. For now, I am surprised to see how well his mental and physical responses are for just coming out of a coma."

David sees father enter the room and calls out, "hey Dad." Dad hugs mom then comes over to give David a hug. He is surprised to hear dad say, "I love you, David, and I thank God that you are all right."

Dad, "God didn't do anything. Love just is."

Dad takes a step back, bewildered by David's response. "Okay, son." He turns to his wife, raises his palms up, and shrugs his shoulders. He whispers to her, "what was that about?" David's mom raised her shoulders and moved her head back and forth.

David turns to the nurse, "You told me you would answer my questions. You asked me what day it was but didn't tell me if I was right."

Nurse Lenus says, "It is Sunday and you have been in a coma for a week. You had an infection called meningitis that affected your brain."

How can that be? I remember everything that has happened since the last time I was in Sunday School. That was when I got into trouble for doubting the existence of God. Hey mom, wasn't that a week ago?"

"Yes, it was," mom replied.

"See nurse Lenus. I can tell you everything that happened in the last week. What would you like to know?"

"OK, David. What did you do on Monday?"

"That's the day that God woke me up and asked if I wanted to play the Love Game. The instructions that God gave me were to go to the park and see how many places I could find God. If I listen with my heart and keep my eyes open, I will hear and see God. He turned to his mom and dad, "I already told you all of this. That's where I met Angela and many others who helped me hear and see God. Don't you remember?"

"So, you saw God," the nurse asks.

"Yes, I did, and have every day since then. I now refer to God as Love."

Nurse Lenus decides not to ask David any more questions. She tells mom and dad on the way out that she will talk to the doctor about getting a psychological consultation.

Mom chooses to stay at the hospital while dad goes home to relieve the babysitter who was caring for David's younger brother. Dad gives me a hug before he leaves and says, "I will pray for you to get better fast."

It wasn't long before a woman wearing a long white lab coat came in. She walks up to David and introduces herself.

"I am Dr. Amara and I'm one of the doctors who have been caring for you this last week. I am a neurologist which means I specialize in illnesses that affect the brain and nerves. I'm happy to see that you are awake. How are you feeling?"

"I was tired when I first woke up but now, I feel good and hungry too."

"The nurse tells me that you are doing well. May I examine you?"

"Sure."

Doctor Amara does the same tests nurse Lenus did plus she checked his reflexes and the sensations in David's feet. "Everything seems fine. There are some other tests we would like to do to make sure there are no long-term problems associated with the infection that we are treating. I am going to have a psychologist see you to check on your mental and emotional health."

"How long do I have to stay in the hospital, Doctor?"

"If all your tests come back normal, then maybe in three days. Your infectious disease doctor will determine when you can go home. Let's first get you some food. We will start slow and see how you do."

"What about the tube in my arm? When will you take it out?"

"You are asking good questions, David. We are still giving you antibiotics through the IV tube and we will continue that until the blood tests are normal and when you are also eating well."

Dr. Amara turned to David's mother and asked her if she had any questions.

Mom said, "not now, but I'm anxious to know what the test results will show."

"Based on the way David is responding this soon after the coma, I am optimistic that he will be fine. I will talk to you when I get the test results. We will schedule the brain scan for tomorrow."

Soon after the doctor left, a nurse's aide walked in with a tray with two plastic containers of Jello, one red and the other green. There was also a small plastic bottle of apple juice. She says, "Let's start with these and I can find something more for you later if you are still hungry. Maybe

144

some ice cream." She gave mom a menu to help me fill out for dinner.

"That sounds good. Thank you."

"You're very welcome, David."

He gobbles up the Jello and the apple juice and follows it with an "ahhhh." He looks at his mom with a smile. Together they looked at the menu for the evening meal. Even though David is hungry, he finds only a few interesting things. He checked the boxes on the menu for hamburgers, french fries, and ice cream. "Mom, I'll pass on the vegetables tonight but maybe you can bring something that I like to eat tomorrow?"

"So, Mom, please tell me what happened. I am so confused. How could I be here a week and have no memory of being in the hospital but I do remember other things."

"It could be that you were dreaming the whole time."

"It seemed so real."

"Honey, sometimes dreams can feel that way. Mom pulls up a chair closer to the bed and begins the story.

Chapter 24

David's Illness

"Last Sunday night you told me you were feeling tired and had a little headache. I felt your head and it seemed you might have a slight fever. I went downstairs to get a Tylenol and water. When I came back you were sound asleep. I left the Tylenol and water on your nightstand. About two in the morning, I woke up suddenly and felt the need to check on you. When I touched your forehead, it felt like you were burning with a fever. I tried to arouse you to give you the Tylenol but you wouldn't wake up. I got your dad up and he called 911. Dad told the operator that you had a high fever and wasn't waking up. She asked if you were breathing OK and Dad told her you were. The operator asked him how far we were from the hospital. He said less than 15 minutes."

"She told him since you were breathing OK, it may be faster if we took you to the hospital ourselves rather than call an ambulance. I woke up Michael to tell him what we were doing and asked him to watch your younger brother until one of us got back. Your dad picked you up and carried you to the car. I sat in the back holding you all the way to the emergency room. The staff took you right away to an exam room and a team of doctors and nurses started their assessment. Since you were unconscious, they asked that we go to the waiting room and they would come and talk to us when they knew something more."

"I hated leaving you but there wasn't anything we could do. It seemed like an eternity but one of the doctors came out about 10 minutes later to tell us they needed to get a brain scan first and then a spinal tap. They suspected meningitis. I asked why you were unconscious and they said that the covering around the brain swells with the infection and puts pressure on the brain. The tests confirmed their suspicion of meningitis and determined it was caused by a bacteria. They started antibiotics right away and sent you to the intensive care unit where you have been in a coma until now. It was a pretty scary experience. The doctors were not very reassuring. They said you might die. I haven't slept much in the last week. Your dad took the week off and we have been taking shifts so one of us was always here.

"How did I get this?"

"You were exposed to someone who carried the bacteria. They might have been in the early stages of getting sick themselves or maybe just carried the bacteria without having symptoms. The doctors couldn't tell us why your body's immune system didn't fight it off before it caused the coma."

"It doesn't matter why, Mom. I accept that it was and at this moment I see everything as perfect. Did this remind you of the feelings you had when I was hospitalized before with pneumonia? You thought I would die then too."

"Yes, it did, but how do you know about that? You were only a year and a half old."

"You told me about it on Wednesday."

"I didn't say anything to you about your pneumonia."

"Mom, you were telling me what the words, "I love you" means to you. You told me how you were raised and had to leave home without finishing eighth grade. You also told me about Michael's alcoholic and abusive father as well as why

148

you had to send Michael away when my father started to physically abuse him. You told me how you had to sneak away with me in the middle of the night to free yourself from my father and his family."

"David, I have never told you those things. How did you know? Who told you?" Was that in your dream?"

"No one told me but you. Maybe it was in a dream. Was it true?"

"Yes, it's true. You're scaring me with what you know about me that I've tried to keep secret."

Mom became very quiet and looked off in the direction of the window. David didn't say anything more either until he realized there was not only a tube coming out of his arm but there was one coming from his penis. "What the hell Mom? What's this thing coming out from below? It's not very comfortable."

"That's the catheter to drain your bladder and measure how much urine you are making."

"Can I get this out so I can get up and go to the bathroom?

"I'll ask the nurse." Mom got up and found nurse Lenus in the hall. "David would like the catheter out so he can use the bathroom. He says it's bothering him. "

"I'll ask Doctor Peros if it is OK for me to remove it. He should be making his rounds soon."

Mom returned to tell David there was another doctor coming soon who would let us know if the catheter could come out.

"Can you find something for me to read or paper to draw on, Mom?

"I'll wait until after the doctor comes, then I will see what they have at the gift shop. Is there anything your dad can bring from home?"

"Yes. He can bring Crystal."

"What is Crystal?"

"That is the beautiful quartz crystal that I found under a rock in the park on Monday. She helped me find and see Love. I left her on the nightstand by my bed."

"David, there is no crystal on your nightstand and you were here last Monday."

"I'll ask Love if what I experienced last week was real or not." "Hey, Love."

"Yes, I AM here."

"Love is here, mom. Did you hear Love say 'I AM here'?"

"I'm sorry I didn't. Why do you call God, Love?"

"God and Love are one and the same. By thinking of God as Love, I am able to go beyond the stories I've been told about God and see Love as the only reality. You don't have to hear or see Love right now. I'll tell you what Love says."

David directs his attention to Love. "Love, is what I experienced last week real? Did I really play the Love Game with you in the park?"

"David tells Mom Love's reply. "What you experienced, David, was absolutely real. The world that you and I created in the last week was just as real as the one your mom experienced. However, it wasn't the same physical world. Remember each person creates their own reality. Your experience in the spiritual world showed you the possibilities that come from listening with your heart and letting your Love-self shine. People may call what you experience an unreal dream. That is just another word to describe a state of being beyond the five senses that they may not value or have not tapped into at this time."

"Where is that coming from David? You are not talking like yourself."

"Like I said Mom, I'm talking with Love. Love talks to my heart and my heart translates Love's message. This can happen only if I'm focused on the present moment and drop any judgments. Love is always here for me and when I don't hear or see Love, it is because I'm covering up my Loveself with fear and judgments."

"Do you see God or Love right now, David?"

"Yes, I see Love when I look at you and I feel perfect." David sees tears in his mom's eyes. "Are you Okay Mom?"

"Wow! To say that I'm feeling wonderful doesn't fully describe the fullness of what I'm experiencing."

"That's Love, Mom. And that is real."

Dr. Peros knocks on the door before coming in. He introduces himself to David. He tells David and his mother that he is very happy that David woke up. He has been

150

looking over the last day's record and says David's progress is going better than expected. "David, how are you feeling right now?"

"At the moment Dr. Peros I am experiencing myself as Love."

"That's an unusual response. I don't think I've ever heard anyone say that before. Do you have any pain?"

"No."

"Any neck stiffness?"

"No."

"Are you still hungry after eating your Jello?"

"Yes, can I have something more?"

"Great, I think we can arrange for you to get something more to eat. Can you sit up for me?

"I think so." David sits up and Dr. Peros checks his heart and lungs.

"Everything sounds good, David."

"When can I get this tube that is down there out?"

"We will get it out today. I would still like to measure your urine output for another day so make sure you pee in the urine container that the nurse will give you." "I would like to keep the IV antibiotics for another few days. Since you are no longer infectious, we can transfer you to a regular room on the pediatric floor tomorrow. Any other questions?

"Can I get out of bed?"

"Yes, as long as someone is with you the first couple of times. Bye now, I will see you tomorrow."

"I really appreciate your care, Dr. Peros. Thank you. See you later."

Mom says, "I notice that everyone who leaves after spending time with you walks out smiling."

Your dad is on his way back and I'm going home to get cleaned up. I think I'm going to be sleeping much better tonight."

"I think I will take a nap for a while."

He noticed the look on his mother's face. "Don't worry, I'm not going back into a coma. Don't forget to get me some paper, maybe some crayons and something to read."

"Ok, I'll be back soon."

Nurse Lenus comes in to take out the catheter. "Are you ready to get rid of this thing?"

"Most definitely. Will this hurt?"

"It may feel weird but it shouldn't hurt." It was out in about 2 seconds.

"You were right, it did feel weird."

You may feel a little discomfort the first time you pee but it should be ok after that."

The nurse gave David the urinal to use when he has to pee... "Remember we need to measure the urine so don't dump it."

Chapter 25

Dream vs Reality

Monday, June 17

"Rise and shine David, It's time to play."

"Hey Love, am I really awake or still in a dream?

"David, my precious player, everything is a dream whether you are awake or sleeping. Dreams are your stories, your imagination, your fantasies, your desires, and the meaning you give to your five senses. Even time and this conversation are dreams. Dreams create the reality of what you call your life. Today is a perfect day to play with the unknowable and embrace the surprises. Observe how your choice of the Game you play adds to your Love story as well as to those around you."

"Ok, Love, I will give it a try."

Lisa, the nurse's aide, says as she comes in with his breakfast. "Good morning, David," "How are you feeling today?"

"Perfect Lisa. How about you?"

"I'm a little tired. Didn't sleep much last night. My daughter Natalie wasn't feeling well."

"Is it alright Lisa if I talk to Love about Natalie? Love is what I call God."

"That would be really nice David. Hope your day goes well. Bye."

"Please wait here for a moment, Lisa."

"Hey Love, is there anything I can do to help Natalie feel better?

David tells Lisa what Love is saying as the message comes through his heart.

"Yes, there is David. Become a Love Lighthouse. Think about Natalie as you open your heart to me so that your LoveSelf shines. That's it. If you judge her illness or suffering as bad and needs to be fixed, you will tumble down the rabbit hole into survival mode. But if you see her as the sparkling Love Star that she is, you might just tickle her heart into a giggle, and abracadabra! A little less shadow, a little more sparkle. This heart-light trick works wonders on any soul swimming in the stormy seas of distress!"

"Thanks, Love, I can do that."

So, Lisa, there you have it from the mouth of Love. What do you think?"

"I don't know what to think. But thank you so much for caring, David. Bye now, I have more breakfasts to deliver." Lisa leaves in a daze.

David finishes his breakfast as the lab technician comes in to draw his blood. She is carrying a tray of empty tubes with rubber stoppers and what looks like syringes without the plungers. "Good morning," David holds his arm out in anticipation and says. "I'm David, what's your name?"

"Good morning to you too. My name is Lily." Lily checks David's ID wristband and says, "You seem pretty relaxed with me taking your blood."

"I'm not afraid. I'm focusing on the present moment instead of imagining fear. Go ahead, do your thing."

"That's amazing that you are able to do that. I worry a lot about lots of things." She is able to get the blood samples easily and then puts a bandage on his arm.

"Lily, Love suggests that I finish living in this moment before trying to live in the future. I forget to do that sometimes. When I worry about something I don't want to happen in the future, I know I am missing the gifts that this moment offers. At least I am aware that I have a choice to keep worrying about things that may never happen or bring myself back to the present moment. It's not always easy but I keep practicing."

"That seems like great advice David. Thanks"

"Lily, When I look into your eyes, I see the Love that you are and it is perfect. Bye now."

Lily leaves wondering how an 11-year-old boy that she has never met before could lighten her day the way David did. She smiles and floats down the hall to her next patient.

Nurse Lenus then enters as if by cue. "How are you today, David?"

"Perfect. How about you?

"Not perfect." Nurse Lenus hangs a small bag containing his antibiotics and connects it to the IV. I am stressed. I have a lot to do and too little time to get it all done."

"That's interesting you say that because that's not what I'm experiencing when I look at you."

"I see you as Love which is perfect."

"I don't think anyone is perfect, David, but thanks for seeing me that way. Would you like to know what is going to happen today?"

"No, I'm playing a Game with Love today where I experiment with how I react to the unknown. "I'm going to let the mystery of each moment unfold just as it is."

"How old are you anyway? You are talking like some old soul."

"My body is 11 but my LoveSelf is really, really old."

"I can believe that. I won't tell you what is going to happen next. Enjoy your game."

David waves to Nurse Lenus as she is leaving then puts his hand over his heart."

She rolls her medication cart back to the nurse's station. She asks those present, "Has anyone talked to David since he came out of his coma?"

Lisa says, "I did. He is not a normal 11-year-old. When I am around him, I feel a lightness in my heart that is hard to describe. He asked permission to talk to God about Natalie who isn't feeling well. Then he goes on to tell me what God said.

Nurse Lenus says, "I agree with you Lisa. Yesterday, he told me that he sees God and that God talks to him. There is a psychiatric consult ordered for today. It will be interesting to see how that goes. David is being transferred out of ICU after his CAT Scan today so we may not see him again.

David hears the usual knocks followed by the door opening. A man pushing a wheelchair comes in. "Hi, I am Josh, and I'm going to take you to get your CAT scan."

"I am David. Are you enjoying your day, Josh?"

"So far it's been great." Josh helps David get into the wheelchair, transfers the IV bags to the pole connected to the chair and they head to the radiology department. On the way, David passes the nurse's station, and the staff, one after another, wish him well. Nurse Lenus says, "I have enjoyed caring for you, David. I'm sure you will have an amazing life."

While waiting for the elevator, David turns and looks straight into Josh's eyes, "what brings you joy?"

"I can't remember anyone asking me that while at work. I enjoy lots of things but most of all I like to write songs and sing them. It is my dream to be in a band, record my songs, or have famous singers sing them."

"Doesn't this job distract you from your calling?"

The empty elevator arrives and Josh and David enter. "David, it does take time away from my writing songs but I need the money to live on until I can get singing jobs."

Josh, I appreciate what you are doing right now, caring for me as I go to get tests. You are providing a valuable service. Are you open to me telling you how I see you from the perspective of Love?"

"Josh's jaw dropped open by this 11-year-old's query. "Sure David, go ahead."

"I wonder if you would be more likely to get singing jobs if you focused your time on writing more songs, getting a band together, and rehearsing? When I looked into your eyes, I saw Love at your core. But it was hiding behind fear, the fear that keeps you from fully committing to your dream of being a singer-songwriter. I bet that if you talked to that Love within you that I see, it might tell you that you are on a journey to create your life as a Love story. It will not use shoulds or shouldn'ts but will invite you to listen with your heart and keep your eyes open. And if you do, your dreams will not only come true but you will also be writing a magnificent Love story of your life."

Josh rolls up to the CT scan waiting room and comes around to face David eye to eye. There was a moment of complete silence as he digested the words, his stillness speaking volumes of his inner turmoil. Finally, Josh asks, "Are you for real?"

"As real as it gets, David says. Thanks for the ride and I'll be waiting for your first album."

"Well, thank you for your perspective. I'll pick you up later, David." Josh shakes his head and wonders, "what the hell just happened?" He walks away deep in thought.

While David waited to be taken into the CAT scan, he wondered whether he should not have offered his perspective to Josh. "Hey Love, was what I told Josh, a reflection of You? I'm not always sure if I should tell someone my feelings or perspectives or not. I don't want them to be upset."

"David, the fact that you did what you did was perfect at that moment as all things are. When you wonder about shoulds or shouldn'ts, you shift to playing the survival game. Ask yourself if that's where you want to be?"

"Love, I didn't think about it beforehand. It just came out."

"From where I'm sitting, you played the Love Game. you saw his fear and your compassion gave him the option to choose to consider hearing your perspective or not. If you were playing the Survival game you might be inclined to try and fix him by preaching what you know. David, you are Love, you don't need to preach it. There will be a time when people will come to you to experience the spirit of Love. Your gift of seeing them as I AM will provide a healing opportunity for those seeking Love, Peace, and Joy. You don't have to do anything more."

A woman wearing blue hospital scrubs comes into the waiting room. "Hi, I AM Sandra. Are you David?" She checks David's ID bracelet.

"Yes, Sandra, I'm David."

"I will be doing your CAT scan today. Please come with me." They walk through the back door of the waiting area to a room with a big machine. David thinks it looks like a giant donut with a table that slides through the opening in its center.

"Do you have any questions about what is going to be happening, David?"

"No questions, Sandra. I would like it if you told me what you were doing as you did it."

"That's fine David. First, get up onto the table and lie on your back. There is the step stool." David climbs up and lies down on the hard cool. table. "I'm going to another room behind that window where the controls are. I will be watching you during the procedure. Okay?"

"Ok, Sandra, this is exciting."

Sandra walks back into the control room. Her voice comes over a speaker in the Cat Scan room, "Can you hear me, David?"

"Yes, I can hear you fine."

"Now the table is going to move you into the center of the CAT Scan machine." David feels only a slight vibration as the table moves him into the donut. It stops when only his head is inside. "It is very important David that you hold very still when the CAT Scan starts. That way we can get the best pictures of your brain. "Ready, hold real still."

"Yep."

David hears a buzzing sound that lasts about 10 seconds. "We're all done, David." The table starts moving again, taking him out of the donut. Sandra comes back in to help David off the table. "You did really well David, I got some good pictures. Not everyone is as relaxed as you are. Your calmness made my job easier." She accompanies David to the waiting room. "Thanks, Sandra for your care."

"You're welcome, David. Have a nice day."

David sits down in one of the chairs and waits for Josh. He imagines sitting by the Peace Pond with Crystal. His thoughts melt away.

"David, are you awake?" David opens his eyes to see Josh.

"I am awake, I was just visiting one of my favorite places." David gets up and settles into the wheelchair.

"That didn't take long, David. How was it for you?"

"It was a breeze."

"I'm still trying to digest what you told me. You said your perspective came from Love."

"Yes, Love is my name for what you may call God. They are the same. I speak from my Loveself which is One within the Divine Love of all existence. You can talk with and hear your Loveself if you quiet your fears and judgments. Quieting your fears and judgments can only be done one moment at a time."

"How do you know this? Did you learn this in church?

"Heaven's no! Like I said, Love told me."

Josh's laughter was tinged with bewilderment as he tried to reconcile his thoughts about David's challenge. "My fears are distracting me from fulfilling my dreams. I want to explore this further. Maybe our meeting today was not an accident and I needed to hear your perspective. For now, I'm going to take you to your new room, new nurses and staff. Are you ready for your new adventure?"

"Perfectly ready Josh."

Chapter 26

Am I Crazy?

"Here we are, David. Your new room," says Josh.

"Thanks, Josh." David then notices his mom. "Hi, Mom, this is Josh. We will be buying his music albums someday. Josh, this is my mom."

"You have quite an insightful son. I really appreciate our short time together. Bye, David."

"Bye, Josh. May your Loveself shine."

David takes a moment to look around the room. No monitors, less noise, nice view out the window, and— "Wow"—a TV.

"How was your morning, David? Are you feeling well? Is there anything I can do for you?"

"No, Mom. I don't need anything. I feel good. You're can relax. The CT scan was an interesting experience. They put me into a big machine. It didn't hurt, and it was over quickly."

An aide comes in carrying a tray. "Hi, David, I'm Cheryl, and I have your lunch. Hope you are hungry. Let me know if you want anything else."

"Thanks, Cheryl. I am really hungry."

David wolfs down his lunch and awaits his next adventure.

A nurse enters with a doctor who David hasn't met before. "I am Barb, the head nurse on this floor, and this is Dr. Deera. He will be talking to you."

Dr. Mark Deera serves as the Chief of Psychiatry at Wellco General Hospital and is the Director of the Behavioral Health Unit. He stands out as a tall, middle-aged figure with distinguished gray at the temples—his presence further accentuated by a consistently professional attire that includes a crisply ironed white shirt, a pale blue patterned tie, and the traditional knee-length white lab coat, but without the usual stethoscope hanging around his neck. His interaction with others is polite and professional, yet he retains a distant air that can intimidate those around him; but he is unaware of this.

"Hi, David, I'm Dr. Deera. I am a psychiatrist and am here to make sure your infection and coma haven't caused any mental or emotional problems. How are you feeling?"

"I think I'm doing really well. How about you?"

"I'm doing well, too. I got a report that you have been seeing and talking to God."

"That's right, Dr. Deera. Aren't you Amma Deera's son, Mark?"

"Yes, I am, David. Do you know my mother?" He looks surprised.

"I thought you looked familiar. I saw your picture with your wife and daughter on the cabinet in Mrs. Deera's dining room. There was also another picture of you with your dad and one with your older sister, Maggie."

"When were you in my mom's house?"

"This past Monday."

"You were in the hospital last Monday, David."

"I know that's what they tell me. Mom says I probably was just dreaming. I saw your mom walking down the sidewalk near the park. She was carrying a bag of groceries

162

in one arm and using her cane in the other. She looked to be struggling, so I decided to help her by carrying the bag home. She invited me into her house and gave me chocolate chip cookies and a glass of milk. She told me this was the first time in a while that she's baked them. She usually made them for Sara."

"Your mom has been feeling lonely after her friend Mary died a couple of months ago. We talked about the game that I was playing with God. I asked if she knew how I could see God. She suggested I let Love guide me. She then gave me a small bag with something in it that might help me. I was told not to open it until I got back to the park. I didn't realize at the time that I was seeing Love—that's what I call God—in her eyes."

"That's quite a dream, David. That doesn't explain how you know about the photos and Sara without actually being in my mom's house."

"I can't explain it, Dr. Deera. I just know it felt real. Love told me that physical and emotional experiences in the spiritual world are absolutely real. I have learned things in the last week that I've never known before. My mom says I know things about her now that have been a secret—things she has never told anyone else about."

"Does God, or Love, have an explanation for that, David?"

"We are all connected by Love, and if I open my heart to the Love that I am, I have access to everything."

"Do you have a clear memory of your experiences in the last week?"

"I can remember everything except being in the hospital."

Dr. Deera completes his mental status exam and tells David everything is fine.

"So, I'm not crazy, Dr. Deera?"

"No, I don't think you are crazy. By the way, in the psychology field, we try to avoid using the word 'crazy.' There are some things that happen that are not explainable in our scientific world. Your story fascinates me. I would like to come back and spend some time with you to get a better understanding of how you experienced what you did. Would you be open to that?"

"Fine with me. Say hi to your mom for me, Dr. Deera. By the way, Love tells me that understanding is overrated. It's what people who are playing the survival game value. But if you enjoy the exploration, I'm here and will support you. I see the Love that you are, and it is perfect."

"Thank you, David. Looking forward to talking to you again. Bye."

Dr. Deera leaves the room and meets with David's mom in the hall. He says, "David doesn't have evidence of psychological issues, although what he knows through his experiences while in a coma is more than a mystery—it is mind-boggling. He even knows things about my mother and daughter. I reassured him that he is not crazy, but I would like to talk to him more. Not because I have to or need to, but because he is just an enchanting young boy with some very mature perspectives. I have evaluated others who have had near-death experiences and come away with some spiritual transformation, but none as profound as David's. I will be back tomorrow if it is okay with you."

Mom says, "Yes, the changes in David are a mystery to me also. It would be nice to have a professional explanation if possible."

Dr. Amara greets Dr. Deera and David's mom in the hall. She informs them that the tentative CT scan was normal and that the full report would be available tomorrow. She asks how Dr. Deera's evaluation of David went. He tells her that his mental status was normal and that he is particularly interested in David's near-death experience and associated insights and will be following up.

"Dr. Amara, I can't thank you enough for the care you provided to David." Mom adds, "I also appreciate the support you offered to me and David's dad when we were so anxious about what was happening in the ICU."

"You're welcome. I am so glad everything turned out fine and that I could contribute to your recovery."

Mom returns to the room and summarizes what doctors Deera and Amara said.

It wasn't long before Dr. Peros and Nurse Barb came in with lab tests. "Everything I tested was normal. I anticipate that we can get the IV out the day after tomorrow. We will keep the IV tube in for the antibiotics, but you don't need the continuous IV solution since you are eating well. Without the bag, you can walk around without the pole. Great news. We also don't have to measure your urine anymore, so you don't have to save it for the nurse. Do you have any questions?"

"No, I don't. This is great news. What about you, Mom?"

"No, I don't have any either."

"I'll check on you tomorrow, David. Take some time to rest. You've had a busy day."

Barb and Dr. Peros left together.

"I'm pretty tired, Mom. I'm going to take a nap before dinner comes."

***

Dr. Deera decides to stop at his mom's house on the way home. He knocks on the door and walks in. "Hey, Mom, you here?" No answer. He calls out a little louder, "Mom, it's Mark, are you home?" He looks around the house and finds it empty. He goes outside and looks down the street to see his mom slowly making her way home. He walks out to meet her.

"What a wonderful surprise, Mark."

"Hi, Mom, where have you been?"

"I started an exercise program."

"Aren't you a little old to start exercising?"

"Are you calling me old?"

"No, I'm sorry. You actually look radiant. I just don't want to see you get hurt. What are you doing?"

"I can tell you; I'm not training for a marathon. This week I've been walking to the park. I sit on one of the benches and feed my friend, Chickadee, then come back. Sometimes, I meet up with my friend Shirley. It takes me about 20 minutes of walking time. I haven't been having as much back pain as I was the week before."

"That sounds like a healthy thing to do."

"I always appreciate you visiting, but I'm curious. What's going on? Why are you here?"

"Can't I just come by for no reason other than I love you?"

"I'm sure you could, but that is not what you tend to do."

Mark opens the door for his mom, and they walk into the kitchen. Mrs. Deera opens her refrigerator and retrieves a pitcher of ice water. "Do you want a glass of water?"

"No, Mom."

She pours a glass for herself and puts the pitcher back in the refrigerator. "Ok, Mark, spill the beans. Why are you here?"

"The strangest thing happened today. I was talking to an 11-year-old boy who just woke up from a coma. He asked me if I was your son. He then told me he recognized me by the picture you have sitting on the dining room cabinet. I asked him if he had been in this house. He said he was last Monday.

"Is your patient's name David?"

"Yes, it is. Do you know him?"

"David was here Monday. He helped me carry my groceries home. He was playing the Love Game with God. I gave him chocolate chip cookies and milk like I used to with Sara. I don't know how, but he knew things about me, Robert, and Mary. I had never met him before. Did he tell you about the birdseed? That was a great idea on my part. He said he fed a chickadee out of his hand. Angela did too, but later in the week."

"Mom, David was in the hospital Monday, in a coma that started Sunday night. He couldn't have been here."

"Mark, I know what I know, and I know he was here. I also saw him with Angela and Roy in the park on Thursday. On Friday, I had a picnic by the Peace Pond with the three of them. We talked about playing the Love Game with a focus on ourselves. It was an extraordinary experience. Have you met Angela yet? She is just as nice and loving as David."

"No, Mom, I haven't. David didn't wake up from his coma until this past Sunday. He couldn't have been in the park when you said you were with him. What did David tell you? He told me the same thing as you. He might have been

166

dreaming about these events when he was in the coma, but that means you would have to have had the same dream. The specific details of both dreams are exactly the same. I've heard of these phenomena happening, but there hasn't been clear documentation. Most people consider it just a coincidence occurring between two people who are very close. Both you and David acknowledge that you have never met before. It's a damn mystery, and I hate mysteries."

"It felt pretty real to me to be a dream. Would you like to have dinner with me tonight since you are already here?"

Dr. Deera hesitated for a moment, thinking about things he had to do, but then said, "Yes, I would love to have dinner with you."

"That makes my day, son."

Mrs. Deera had taken homemade spaghetti sauce out of the freezer earlier in the day, and it had almost thawed. She puts it in a saucepan on the stove at low heat. She fills a large pot with water to cook the pasta. She carries it to the stove, adds a perfect amount of salt, and turns the heat up to high.

"Mom, what else happened with David?"

"I had a moment with him when we looked into each other's eyes. An intense, indescribable feeling surged through my body. He told me that it was no accident we met because God wanted to relay a message to me through him. The message was that God was here for me and has always been—through the death of your father and my friend Mary. God has not abandoned me, but my grief closed my heart to His presence. Maybe that surge of emotion was God's presence. I know that I have never felt the same since that day or dream with David."

Mrs. Deera stirred the spaghetti sauce, turns up the heat, swings around, and takes salad makings out of the fridge. She grabs a couple of bowls from the cabinet for the salad.

"Mom, you move around the kitchen so effortlessly. You look like you are dancing."

"Experience, son, experience."

"Then you saw David again later in the week?"

"Yes. I was exercising like I told you and went to the park to feed Chickadee. I had the urge to take one of the sidewalks off the main road. I'm not really sure why I was drawn to take this new path. It took me to an unfamiliar part of the park, and that's when I saw David with a young girl and a homeless man. I put some money in his 'help can.' David gave me a big hug and introduced me to Angela and Roy. They were telling Roy how to play the Love Game. Then Angela and David accompanied me as I headed home. Before going our separate ways, we stopped and had a silent moment looking into each other's eyes. That's when I heard Love speak."

"What do you mean, Mom?"

"I heard, 'I AM here,' as plain as day. It sounded like my own voice, but I didn't say it. David and Angela heard it at the same time. They each heard it as their own voice. I was overcome by an indescribable feeling that I experienced as perfect. It was even more profound this time compared to the feeling I had with David alone. I think everything was magnified when there were three of us with open hearts at the same moment. This is the effect of Love. I kept chuckling in disbelief the rest of the way home. Well, in all my years, I have never experienced such a moment. I have more energy than I've had in quite a while."

"That's amazing, says Mark.

"Like I said, the feelings I had were so real I didn't think of it as a dream. I did become suspicious that something crazy was going on when I heard on the Friday evening news that a veteran named Roy was discovered dead in his motel room early that morning. They showed a picture of Roy, and it was the same man we had the picnic with after they said he died. They said he died of natural causes. What do you make of that?"

"I don't know, Mom. It's just another thing adding to the mystery of how all this is happening. It certainly challenges my scientific beliefs."

She drains the pasta, puts it on a plate, and adds the sauce. She reaches into the refrigerator for the Parmesan and the salad dressing. Mrs. Deera completes her dance by cutting a few slices off a baguette and putting them on a plate with a side of butter. "Now we can eat."

"Mom, this is fantastic."

"Mark, you've heard all about my adventures. How are you doing?"

"I've been a little lonely since Sara left for school, but I'm keeping pretty busy at work."

"It's been a couple of years since your divorce. Are you dating anyone?"

"No. You don't know how hard it is to meet people who aren't patients or hospital staff. Plus, I'm hesitant to risk another failed relationship."

"Are you doing anything that brings you joy?"

"Not much. I might have been having some mild depression. That was until earlier today when my energy really perked up after meeting David. I was intrigued by his story, and now after hearing your side of your shared dream, I'm excited to explore this phenomenon more. I also want to know more about Angela and how she fits into the picture. Is she real or made up in David's and your dream world?"

"It's been hard for me, Mark, to separate what is real and what is a dream. They seem to overlap. What I do know is that the perfect feeling I had was real."

"Thanks so much for dinner, Mom. I have some additional things I want to get done before I go to bed." Dr. Deera gives his mom a hug and says, "I love you, Mom. I want to talk to you again when I know a little more of David's story."

"I love you too, Mark. And you don't have to wait for an agenda before spending time with me."

Chapter 27

It's a Mystery

Tuesday, June 18

David's mom arrives and finds him sitting up in the chair, eating his breakfast, while Cheryl, the nurse's aide, changes his bed. "Good morning, David," she says, giving him a hug and a kiss. "How are you feeling today?"

"Great. I'm feeling more and more energy every day. Plus, no tests today."

Nurse Barb and Dr. Amara come in. While the nurse connects a bag of antibiotic solution to his IV line, Dr. Amara gives David and mom an update on the CAT Scan's final report. She says everything is normal. She tells them that since David is doing so well, it won't be necessary for her to see him anymore.

David's mom thanks Dr. Amara again for the good care she provided, not only to David but also to her and David's dad.

Dr. Peros enters with Nurse Barb on his heels. "How are you doing today, David?"

"Great. I feel back to normal."

"That's wonderful. Your last antibiotic treatment will be tomorrow at noon. You can go home after that dose is complete. You will need to follow up with your pediatrician in about a week."

Barb reminds Dr. Peros, "David hasn't had a bowel movement since he was admitted. What do you want to do?"

"Let's give him a laxative, and if that doesn't work, I'll order an enema. I'll see you tomorrow morning, David. Bye now."

Nurse Barb says, "Maybe a little activity will help your bowels move, and we won't have to give you an enema."

David scrunches his face. "Ooh, I'm all for avoiding an enema. Mom, let's take a walk."

Before they get out the door, Dr. Deera comes in. David notices the excitement in his eyes and says, "You must be having a good day."

"I am, David. I really am. Please sit down; I want to talk to both of you. Yesterday, David mentioned my mom and said he dreamt about being in her house. That's how he knew I was her son. So, I visited my mom last night to ask her if she knew you. To my surprise, she had the same dream as you did. All the details were there. She said she visited with you again later in the week."

David interrupts, "Yes, on Thursday and Friday."

"Yes, that's what she said too. She said that's when she met Angela and Roy. I'm curious—who is Angela? Is she real, or just a character in your shared dream?"

"I never met Angela before this last week. I don't know anything about her other than what she and her nana told me in my dream."

"My mom tells me you told her about the Love Game and that it has changed her life," says Dr. Deera. "What is that about?"

"The Love Game is what God woke me up last Monday to play. I was doubting the existence of God because I couldn't see Him, and He wouldn't talk to me. God wanted me to get to know Him more. To play the game, I was invited to go to the park and see how many places I could find Him. I was told if I listened with my heart and kept my eyes open, I would actually see God."

"As it turned out, I had a lot of trouble seeing God because of my expectations and beliefs. Chickadee shifted my perspective from searching for God to searching for Love since they were one and the same. With the help from many Love beings I encountered, I was finally able to hear, see, and experience multiple perfect forms of Love. Angela is an angel who helped me."

Dr. Deera says, "This is so fascinating, David. It's a mystery that I'm excited to explore further, especially how multiple people seem to be sharing the same dream. My mom told me that you all met with Roy at the Peace Pond later Friday morning. Did you know that he was found dead in his motel room earlier that morning before you met with him?"

"I didn't know that, Dr. Deera. I know it must have been a dream, but he seemed alive and well to me. We had a really good time discussing the challenge of seeing ourselves as Love when we don't like who we are, what we look like, or what we've done."

"It's close to lunch. How about I treat you and your mom to lunch in the coffee shop?"

David looks toward his mom, who smiles and nods her head. "Sure, that would be great, Dr. Deera."

On the way, they happen to walk by a room with an open door when they hear someone calling out, "David, hey DavidLove, is that you?"

David turns to see a young girl sitting up in bed. Mom and Dr. Deera freeze as David runs into the room.

"Angela, you're here. I can't believe it's really you." David holds Angela's face. "Let me look into your eyes. Yes, it's you. I see the Love that you are, and I feel perfect."

Mrs. Walden and Dr. Deera share a look of sheer bewilderment. They slowly walk through the door as David and Angela are hugging. Nana Sage springs from her seat, letting her knitting fall to the floor, her eyes wide with shock at the exchange between David and Angela.

"I am Dr. Deera, and this is David's mom, Victoria."

"I am Nana Sage, Angela's grandmother. What's going on here?"

"Nana, this is David, the person I have been playing in the park with this last week. I told you we were playing the Love Game. He is also the boy in the tree that I drew the picture of."

"This is the David? I thought you were dreaming, Angela."

"Well, we were dreaming. We were dreaming together."

Pointing to Dr. Deera, David says, "Angela, do you know who this is?" Angela shakes her head no. "It's Mrs. Deera's son, Dr. Mark Deera."

"Oh, nice to meet you. I really enjoy being with your mom, Dr. Deera."

"My mom told me about you last night." He then turns to Nana Sage and tells her, "Apparently, my mom and the two of them have been sharing dreams about playing the Love Game in the park."

"I've never heard of such a thing," Nana says.

Dr. Deera says, "There is very little published in the literature about this kind of shared dreaming. What is even more unusual is that they didn't know each other before the dream, and they all dreamt that God talked to them, using the same words at the same time."

David leans over to Nana and whispers to her, "Nana, you were in my dream too, and you told me about the time when you were a young girl alone in the woods. You said you had an out-of-body experience and later learned it was Divine Spirit entering your body."

Nana says back to David in her normal voice, "I told you that? I've never told anyone that before."

Angela asks David, "What are you doing here?"

"I've been in the intensive care unit for the last week in a coma. I had meningitis. I'm better now, and you can't get what I had. They say I can go home after my last antibiotic dose tomorrow."

"I missed seeing you the last two days, DavidLove."

"Yeah, I missed you too."

Dr. Deera says, "Your mom and I are going to get something to eat. Would you like to come, David?"

174

"No, I want to stay with Angela."

"How about you, Mrs. Sage?"

"Please, my friends call me Nana. Yes, I would like to. Let the kids have some private time."

Dr. Welling, Angela's oncologist, was passing by the room as Dr. Deera was leaving with the two women. "Mark, I'm surprised to see you here. Is something wrong?"

"No, on the contrary, everything is perfect. I invite you to go in and meet Angela's friend, David. I'll talk to you later about the mystery of their relationship. We're going down to get something to eat."

"I'm intrigued. Talk to you later." Dr. Welling goes in to talk to the two kids.

"Hi, Dr. Welling. This is my best friend, DavidLove. Love isn't his last name, but that's what I call him because he has an open heart, and I can see the love that is him. DavidLove, this is Dr. Welling; she is the doctor treating my cancer."

"Hello, Dr. Welling."

"Hello to you too, David. I saw Dr. Deera in the hall, and he said the two of you have a mysterious relationship. How long have you known each other?"

Angela says, "It's hard to answer. We first met last week in the park and have been playing there since."

"Angela, you haven't been out of the hospital in the last week."

"I know. I'm told we were dreaming together. We met for the first time outside the dream world in the last half hour."

"I was in a coma for a week in the ICU until I woke up Sunday," David says. We discovered each other by accident today. Dr. Deera thinks the only explanation is dream-sharing. It is a mystery because we have never seen or interacted with each other until last week. What really boggles his mind is that we have also been dream-sharing with his mother, whom we haven't met yet in person. Love—or what you might call God—invited us to play the Love Game, and that Game seems to be connecting us. We have stories about everywhere we have seen Love."

"Sounds fascinating, David. It's beyond anything I've experienced before. I can see why Dr. Deera, as a scientist, may find it difficult to explain how this can happen. I'm interested to get his take on your ability to connect so deeply. Angela, I did notice a significant improvement in your mood in the last week. Maybe your new friends have something to do with that change. I hope you two have as much fun playing in awake time as you did in dreamtime. Bye."

Dr. Deera, David's mother, and Nana were enjoying their lunch in the Wellco Cafe. A corner table offered them some privacy. Dr. Deera says, "I'm really glad to have the chance to talk to you about David, Angela, and my mother. Sometimes things that are really unexplainable happen and leave us all scratching our heads. It isn't just that they are sharing dreams; it's the very positive effect they are having on those around them. I've been talking to the staff about David, and everyone who has had contact with him leaves feeling better. I just met Angela, so I haven't talked to the staff about her effect on them, but I suspect the spiritual nature of the game they have been playing will yield the same results. My mother tells me she has felt significantly better physically and emotionally since having these dreams. What have the two of you noticed in the last week?"

Vicki spoke first. "Of course, I didn't know what was happening while David was in the coma. Soon after he woke up, he was telling me some things about my life that I haven't told anyone before. He said that I told him that information in a dream. I have noticed a change in his behavior since waking up. He was shy and self-conscious before; now, I see confidence in the way he interacts with others. He shows a genuine interest in others, asking them questions about their lives. Before getting sick, he would engage in conversations only when others started them. If someone asked him something he was excited about, you couldn't shut him up. What's a mystery to me is where the spiritual perspective he has been telling me about is coming from. They don't teach his philosophy in Sunday School."

"What about you, Nana? Has Angela changed in the last week? Dr. Deera inquired.

"She has been sleeping more in the last week. She tells me about her dreams, so I knew about David as well as your mother, Dr. Deera. I initially wondered if it was an effect of her cancer progressing and involving her brain. Her optimism and appreciation of each moment seemed to increase in the last week. She talked to me about the three levels of the Love Game and that she was practicing Level 3 with David."

"I didn't know anything about that, Vicki says."

Nana says, "Victoria, David had been in a coma for the last week while Angela was awake, so she told me each day what was happening. I'm sure David would jump at the chance to talk about his perspectives and experiences with the Love Game."

Victoria followed by saying to Nana, "Please call me Vicki." "You're probably right, Nana. I've been focusing so much on what is happening now with his health that I may not have given him much opportunity to talk about his dreams. I think his father hasn't either. I think he might have avoided talking to David because David's spiritual perspectives seem to conflict with his beliefs."

Dr. Deera said, "Already my life, my beliefs, and how I want to show up in this world have taken on new meaning in the last 24 hours. I want you to know that I'm here for you both. Thanks for sharing this time with me. I have an appointment I want to get to now. I will see you tomorrow. Bye."

Nana and Vicki finished their lunch and went back to Angela's room.

"David, I don't think you need me hanging around. I will leave you two alone and will be back tomorrow morning," says his mom.

"Angela, I'm going to go home a little early to be with Sammy," says Nana. "David, I trust that you will go back to your room if Angela gets too tired."

"Certainly, Nana." David turns to Angela. "You will let me know if you want me to go, right?"

"Of course, DavidLove."

Vicki and Nana walked out together, smiling about the connection these two eleven-year-olds have. They stopped at the nurses' station to let the nurses know that it's okay with them that Angela and David are spending time together. Even halfway down the hall, they could hear

Angela and David laughing. The nurse then said, "They are the best medicine for each other."

Vicki and Nana simultaneously said, "I agree."

"DavidLove, I have something that is really bothering me. I haven't seen Sammy for almost two weeks now. We are so close. We've gone through so much together. I would take care of him when Momma wasn't around or when she was drunk. Momma abandoned him, and now I have too. I worry about how he is feeling. Is he scared? Is he feeling alone? Nana has been spending so much time with me, maybe he feels abandoned by her too. Does he even understand what is happening and that I might die? What can I do? How can I help him? What if we could include him in our dreams? Do you think that would help? DavidLove, I need to see Sammy. I want to comfort him. What can we do to make that happen? Am I playing the survival game right now?"

David holds Angela's hand and listens in silence throughout her parade of questions. He follows with a question of his own. "Would you consider offering all these questions to the Peace Pond and seeing what surfaces in your heart overnight? While you are waiting for some direction, would you consider creating some perfect feelings for yourself right now?"

"I can, DavidLove, thank you." Angela picks up her journal and starts drawing.

The nurse comes in and asks David to go back to his room so they could give him his next IV antibiotic treatment. His dinner would be there soon after. David gives Angela a hug and whispers to her that he too will offer her questions to the Pond."

Chapter 28

Dream-Sharing

Wednesday, June 19

"DavidLove, wake up."

"Is something wrong, Angela?"

"Nothing's wrong. Can you sneak into my room? I want to be with you."

"Okay, I'm on my way."

David looks out into the hall. Everything is quiet, including the irritating monitors in some patients' rooms. The two night nurses and the aide are talking in the break room behind the nurse's station.

David crouches down as he passes the nurses' station and continues to Angela's room. He snuggles up to Angela on the bed and gives her a kiss.

"Thanks for coming," Angela whispers. "I was at the Peace Pond and got a message about Sammy."

"Me too, Angela. Go ahead with yours. What did you receive?"

"I think my idea about inviting Sammy to dream with us may ease my concerns."

"I received the same message, Angela."

"But, DavidLove, we've never controlled who does or doesn't dream with us. Our dream buddies just happen mysteriously."

"I know, Angela, but we have never really tried to see if we could. I don't think it's about trying to control his dreams. We need to get in our LoveSelf space and invite him to join us. It would be great for you if he does, but if he doesn't, that will be okay too because another way will appear. I remember Love saying that the universe will support our desires if we are aligned with our LoveSelves. I know you can create the reality of you and Sammy communicating with each other. Maybe if we both hold that intention, we'll make it happen. Has Sammy come to the hospital to see you?"

"He hasn't. I think he is afraid of hospitals."

"I think we could get him to dream-share with us if you had the chance to talk to Sammy directly. I bet he would jump at the chance to play the Love Game with us."

"I'll go now, and I'll be back after my morning IV treatment, Angela."

"Before you leave, DavidLove, please get in bed with me and hold me like you did in the woods?"

"I would like that, but are you sure? This isn't a dream."

"It is for me. I may not have any more opportunities to feel the pleasure of you holding me." Angela wraps her arms around David.

Carolyn, the night nurse, walks by the room and hears Angela and David talking. She knocks on the door. David immediately ducks under the covers. Carolyn sticks her head into the dark room. "Angela, who were you talking to? Are you okay? I thought I heard David's voice."

"I'm fine, I was just praying."

Carolyn scans Angela's room. "Fine. Call if you need me." She was still shaking her head when she arrived back to the nurse's station.

180

"The weirdest thing just happened," she says to Linda, the other nurse on duty. "I was walking by Angela's room and I swore I heard Angela and David talking. When I looked in the room, Angela was alone."

Linda responds, "I just checked on David about five minutes ago and he was sound asleep. You must have been dreaming."

David sticks his head out from under the sheet. "Holy crap, I thought for sure she could hear my heart pounding. I'd better go."

"DavidLove, wait a few minutes before you leave to give her a chance to get back to the nurse's station. I would really enjoy it if you just held me in the meantime."

David was able to make it back to his room undetected. He couldn't stop smiling as he replayed his time with Angela and the perfect feeling they shared.

Nurse Barb wakes up David to attach the antibiotic bag to the IV line. "Good morning. Please give me a moment to go to the bathroom," David says. He goes to the bathroom, pees, washes his hands, splashes his face with water, and smiles at the image of Love reflected in the mirror.

"Isn't it a great day, my lovely nurse?"

"Yes, David. This is the day you break out of here. We will certainly miss your charm and loving presence." She checks his pulse, temperature, and respirations. "Everything is normal." She assures the IV is flowing well, then starts the antibiotic.

Cheryl brings David his breakfast. "Cheryl, don't you have a family gathering this weekend at your house?"

"I do. I am surprised. I don't remember telling you that. I am excited to see my daughter, who is home on leave from the army. It's been six months since I last saw her. I'm taking Friday off to start preparing."

"I'm sure you will have an awesome time. I'll be around tomorrow with Angela, so I will stop by to say goodbye. Thank you so much for your care, Cheryl. I really appreciate the Love that you are. Can I have a hug?" David asks as he looks deep into Cheryl's eyes.

"You most certainly can." She gives him a hug and experiences the Perfect 'wow' feeling. "See you later," she says as she walks out of the room with her hand over her heart.

Dr. Peros comes in with Barb. "Good morning, young man. How are you feeling today?"

"I am perfect Love."

"I suppose there can't be any better way to feel. I have written the discharge orders for later. Barb will give all the written instructions to your mom when she comes in. It has been a pleasure caring for you, David."

"I feel so privileged to have someone like you taking care of me when I was at death's door, Dr. Peros. I will be forever grateful. Words aren't enough." David looks deep into his eyes as he crosses his hands over his heart. David then extends his hands, palms up, toward Dr. Peros. "May I give you a hug?"

"I would like that, David." Barb notices tears welling up in the doctor's eyes as he and David connect. She gives Dr. Peros a knowing touch on his shoulder as they leave. On the way back to the nursing station, he asks her, "What just happened? I've never had that kind of reaction to a patient."

"You've never had a patient like him before."

Once the IV was done, David hurried to Angela's room. He felt lucky that he made it in time to see Dr. Welling with Angela.

"Dr. Welling, can David and my brother Sammy visit me at the same time?"

"It's OK as long as an adult is present."

"Great! We have to call Nana right away to ask her to bring Sammy. Would you take care of that for me, DavidLove?"

David does. "Nana, Angela would really like you to bring Sammy with you when you come. Dr. Welling said it was Okay."

"I think that is a good idea, David. I'll get Sammy ready, and we will be there soon."

When Sammy enters the room, he blurts out, "Angela, you've lost so much weight. You look terrible."

"Nice to see you too, Sammy. Come over and give me a hug."

Sammy gives her a hug and apologizes. 'I'm sorry I said that, Angela. I wasn't expecting to see you so sick."

"I know, a lot has happened in the ten days since I saw you last. I want you to meet David. He is my best friend, and we have been helping each other find Love.'

"Hey, Sammy."

"Yeah, hey, David."

Nana gives Angela a hug and turns to David to give him one too.

"Sit down, Sammy. David and I want to talk to you about dreaming together. We think it will be really important for you to know what is happening in case I don't get better."

"I don't understand, Angela. What do you mean if you don't get better? You're going to beat this cancer. What do you mean by dreaming together?"

"It is a way to connect and talk to each other when we are not physically present."

"You mean like talking on the phone?"

"No, Sammy. It's like when you see and talk to people in your dreams at night. Only, we are having the same dream at the same time. It can seem very real. David and I want to teach you how to be a part of our dream-sharing with Love. Love is what we call God. You won't have any nightmares or bad dreams when we allow Love to be present."

"I don't know, Angela. This sounds kind of weird."

"It's definitely weird and unusual, Sammy, but in the coming days, I feel it will be really important for you to tap into what I am experiencing. I want you to know that this is just an invitation, not something that you have to do. By the way, this is for you too, Nana."

"Angela, I have seen the effects that dream sharing has had on you and David, so you can count me in," says Nana.

"David, please explain to Nana and Sammy how to connect through our dreams."

David tells them, "Divine Love is a part of us and is always present within our heart and connects us to all that exists. It is our Loveself. When we dream share, it is actually this Loveself that is dreaming. Our intention then is to open our hearts to our Loveself and let them do their thing."

David goes on to tell Sammy and Nana how to play the Love Game to help them open their hearts.

David's mom appears at the open door to Angela's room. "I thought I would find you here. Hi, everyone."

"Mom, this is Sammy, Angela's brother. Sammy, this is my mom."

"Nice to meet you, Sammy. David, Nurse Barb wants to go over the discharge instructions with the two of us. Then you can have your lunch and the last IV treatment."

"Okay, Mom." David hugs Angela. "Bye, Love. I'll see you later."

"I feel like taking a nap now anyway. See you later, DavidLove."

Soon after David leaves, Angela falls asleep. Nana looks over to Sammy, and he too is asleep. She puts her knitting down, leans back in her chair, and nods off.

Angela is sitting at the Peace Pond when Sammy and Nana show up. "Thanks for coming to this special place," Angela says.

"What is this place?" Sammy asks.

"This Pond is where you can come to release judgments and open your heart to your Loveself. You can offer the pond your stresses and fears, and it will show you Love. This is where David first realized he was looking at Love, and you will too. You will know when your Loveself is shining by the perfect feeling you will experience. How do you guys feel right now?"

Nana and Sammy sit on the edge of the pond and gaze into its depths. Nana's eyes close for a moment, and when she opens them, she finds herself high in the sky, looking down at the trio. She rose up higher and higher until she could see the whole park and then the city. This reminds her of the out-of-body experience she had as a child. Instead of looking at a few puzzle pieces, she started seeing much more of the picture. The feeling was wonderful and perfect.

"Is this the beauty that God sees?" she wonders.

"I AM here. I AM the Pond. I AM the beauty, and I AM Love. I AM also you, Nana, and you, Angela, and you too, Sammy. Rejoice, we are One Love."

184

Sammy grasps Angela's hand in surprise at the voice of Love. Angela tells him this is what perfection is all about. Nana is back in her body, and the three sit in silence, basking in the Light radiating from their hearts. Chickadee flies down and sits on Angela's hand. "I was drawn to your Light and came to visit," says Chickadee. "Hi, Angela. How are you guys doing?"

"Hi, Chickadee. This is my Nana and brother, Sammy."

Sammy's mouth drops open as he stares at Chickadee. "What the heck?" he says.

Chickadee invites Nana and Sammy to hold out their hands. Two more Chickadees land on their outstretched hands. "These are my chicks that David and Angela provided food for."

Nana and Sammy were mesmerized by the connection they felt looking into the eyes of these young birds. "I AM here."

Nana and Sammy simultaneously say, "I see you."

"Thank you so much for sharing your family with us," says Angela.

"And thank you for sharing your Loveselves. It's time to go, kids." Chickadee and her young ones flew off, leaving awestruck smiles behind.

When they return from the Pond, they open their eyes to see David waiting for them. "I didn't want to disturb you in the middle of your dream. How was it?"

"I had a really weird but nice dream," says Sammy. "I was at a pond when a bird landed on my hand."

"We all had the same dream, David. And guess what? Chickadee came with her two chicks," says Angela.

"I wish I was there. So, Sammy and Nana, you now know what dream sharing is about."

"It blows my mind trying to understand how this can happen," says Nana.

"You don't need to understand in order to accept the Perfection of your experience."

"I'm going home now. I'll be back tomorrow." David gives Angela a kiss on her mouth and whispers, "I'll see you in our dreams."

Sammy's eyes open wide with a slight twist of his mouth at the unexpected display of affection. Nana just smiled.

David's mom appears at the door. "Are you ready to go, David?"

"Yeah, Mom." David waves to Angela as he backs out of the room.

Angela continues her routine of napping, dreaming, and drawing for the rest of the day.

Chapter 29

Radiant Love-selves

Thursday, June 20

Nana and Sammy pick up David at his house. They will spend the day together with Angela.

Nurse Barb comes into Angela's room to find both David and Angela lying in the bed next to each other. "What are you two doing," she barks? "David, you shouldn't be in bed with Angela. Now, please get out. You can sit in the chair."

David asks, "Why?"

"It's just not right."

"What are you afraid of? We're not going to have sex in the hospital, especially not in front of Nana and Sammy. We would do it more secretly, like we did last week in the woods." The nurse's jaw falls open in shock. Nana is just as surprised. Sammy, with smiling eyes, looks up from his video game. There is a moment of silence before the kids break out laughing.

Angela stops laughing long enough to ask the nurse, "Really, what harm will it do? We enjoy being next to each other. Wouldn't you like someone close to you if you were dying?"

The nurse stutters, "I suppose so." When she turns to walk out, she notices Nana sitting in the corner chuckling. Nurse Barb says, "I was never here," then walks out.

David turns to Angela. "Did she just lie that she was never here?"

"Yeah, but it was a perfect one," Angela says.

"I can't believe you used the dying con."

"It's not a con, DavidLove. They haven't told me yet, but I know I am dying."

"How do you know that?" asks David.

"I just know."

Angela's revelation felt like a slap in the face to David. Nana jumps out of her chair, comes over to the bed, and tells Angela, "Child, don't give up hope. You are going to be fine. You have to continue fighting this cancer."

"Angela, I don't want you to die," says Sammy, with tears in his eyes.

"No matter what happens, everything is perfect." Even though Angela knew she was dying, she didn't want to squash Nana's and Sammy's hope. Nana goes back to her chair to finish knitting a new hat for Angela.

David looks into Angela's eyes. "I know we talked about the possibility of you dying, but this seems more of a certainty. Angela, I don't want you to die. I don't know what else to say."

"DavidLove, let's just focus for the moment on creating our Love stories."

"I don't know if I am ready for that. I just fell into the survival game."

"Remember when Butch bullied me? I helped you switch back to the Love Game, and I can do it again." Angela calls out, "Hey Love, we need some guidance turning this situation back into a Love Story." Angela gets Love's message. She puts her hands on each side of David's face and looks into his eyes. "I see the Love you are, and I feel

188

perfect. Whatever game you want to play, I will still see you as perfect."

David takes a breath. "Angela, that is part of the problem I am creating. I'm telling a story that you won't be here when I need you. Just by touching my face, I felt the presence of Love. I fear that I will never find someone like you to lift me up."

Angela responds, "Don't you remember that you were the one who introduced me to Love? You taught me the Love Game. You saw the Light, and you will never be able to forget it. So, if you close your heart, it won't be for long. Love will remind you, 'I AM here.'"

Even though Angela was focusing on David, when she said, "I see the Love you are," both Nana and Sammy felt a sudden feeling of joy rush through them.

"I AM here." Love then says, "Let me reassure you that what you are experiencing is perfect. Each of you has been offered gifts of acceptance, hope, resistance, denial, and grief before you. These experiences will help guide you to the truth of Love and the realization that there is nothing that is ever lost."

"Something the four of you aren't fully aware of is how your radiant Loveself facilitates others to open their hearts. When this happens, the consciousness of all existence is elevated. The power of your Divine Light is magnified many times when multiple Loveselves are radiating together like the four of you. Rejoice."

David and Angela laugh when Nana says, "Amen."

David gets up and tells Angela, "I will be back in a little while. I want to go talk to Dr. Deera." He then goes to the nurse's station.

"I see you got out of bed, David," Nurse Barb says. "What can I help you with?"

David smiles and says, "I thought you didn't see me in the bed." Barb smirks with a half-smile.

"I would like to know how to get to Dr. Deera's office."

"You'll have to take the elevator to the third floor and follow the signs to the medical office building. You'll cross a bridge that connects the buildings to the hospital. Once you're there, just look at the directory for his office number."

"I got it. Thanks. I also want to thank you for not kicking me out of Angela's bed. It really means a lot to me to be close to her."

David follows Nurse Barb's directions to the directory in the office building. "OK, there it is, Dr. Mark Deera, suite 303." He opens the door into an empty waiting room. He walks up and knocks on the window at the back of the room. A woman opens the window and says, "Hello, can I help you?"

"Hi, I'm David. I would like to see Dr. Deera."

"Do you have an appointment?"

"No, I don't, but I saw him yesterday in the hospital, and I have something important to ask him."

"He is with a patient right now. He should be done in about 10 minutes. I will ask him then if he will see you."

"Thanks, I can wait." Sitting, David scans the stark waiting room. There are three chairs—one group of two separated by a small table between them. A few magazines rest on top. Nature photos adorn the walls. One photo reminds him of Peace Pond, another of a trail going through a beautiful forest. The trees looked too big to climb. The last photo is of the seashore at sunset. He wonders if Dr. Deera intentionally chose the photos for their calming effect or if he is just a nature person. There is a National Geographic magazine on a small table next to the chair he is sitting on. He picks it up and starts flipping through the pages, focusing on the photos. He doesn't get far into the magazine when Dr. Deera opens the office door next to the receptionist's window.

"David, I'm surprised to see you. I have only a few minutes. What can I do for you?"

"I would like to ask you for a big favor."

"Go for it, David."

"Angela's momma, Rachel, is in the hospital across town. She is being treated in the psychiatric unit. Nana Sage said Rachel became depressed after Angela was diagnosed with cancer. She began drinking more and more alcohol to ease her pain. After Rachel got drunk and started throwing things in the house, Nana asked her to leave. Nana feared her drinking would cause more serious problems for the children. It was okay with Rachel because being around Angela seemed to distress her more. A few weeks ago, she was taken to the emergency room after overdosing on pills and alcohol. She said she didn't want to live anymore. They admitted her for treatment and suicide monitoring."

"Angela is dying, Dr. Deera. I don't know how long she will live, but it may be only a few days. Do you think you could have her momma transferred over here temporarily and help her to be able to see Angela before she dies? Angela is so connected to Love right now that it may help her mom heal. I know Angela forgives her momma for leaving when she most needed her. How do you feel about being a part of Angela and Rachel reconnecting? I'm sure it would also help Nana Sage and Rachel's relationship too."

"This is really unusual for this to happen because of administrative obstacles. I can't force Angela's mother to consent to the transfer, and I can't promise that it will happen even if she consents. I am willing to try. I'll start by calling my friend who directs the psychiatric unit."

"Thank you so much, Dr. Deera. I have a feeling that the obstacles are going to melt away."

David then goes back to Angela's room.

Dr. Deera returns to his office and calls Dr. Bill Shapiro.

"Hey, Bill, Mark here. I understand you have a patient over there by the name of Rachel Sage. Her 11-year-old daughter, Angela, is dying of cancer. From what I understand, much of Rachel's depression was triggered by Angela's condition. I know this is an unusual request, but is Rachel stable enough to see her daughter before she dies, and would you consent to transferring her here either temporarily or permanently under my care?"

Bill tells Mark that they are bursting at the seams in the psych unit. Rachel has been taking her meds and making progress. She is stable at the moment, but she also isn't aware of Angela's current status. He will ask Rachel if she is willing to be transferred to Mark's care. They will have to discharge her from there and have a security guard accompany her until she is admitted to Mark's facility. Bill asks Mark if he will care for Rachel until she is ready to be discharged.

"Yes, I will. If Rachel is in agreement, would you handle the transfer details, Bill? I will take care of the admission on this end."

Dr. Shapiro asks his secretary, "Please call Jeanie, the charge nurse, and ask her to take Rachel to the counseling room in 10 minutes. Tell her that I will meet them there."

Rachel and Beverly were already sitting down when Dr. Shapiro entered the room. He sat in the desk chair facing them. A small desk was beside him. "How are you feeling today, Rachel?"

"I feel like I am getting better every day. Is something wrong? I wasn't expecting a private session with you today."

"I got a call from Dr. Mark Deera, who is the chief of psychiatry at Wellco General. He asks if you are willing to be transferred to their unit, and he would take over your care. If you're interested, he would support you so that you could visit with your daughter in the pediatric unit. He says she is pretty sick. Are you open to his invitation?"

"I don't know if I can handle facing her. I feel so ashamed for leaving her. What kind of scum mother would abandon her child when she most needed love? My depression got worse the longer I stayed away. The alcohol couldn't numb me enough. Yes, I'm feeling a little better now, but I worry I will slip back if I see her. She is such a beautiful and loving child. She doesn't deserve me."

"Rachel, I will support you regardless of your decision. I'm also not going to tell you that you should or shouldn't go. I will tell you that Dr. Deera is an excellent doctor, and there is no one better to help you reconnect with your daughter. If your daughter dies, he will be there to help you through the grieving process. Take some time to think about it, but not too long because I will need some time to make arrangements if you decide to go. Is that okay?"

"Yeah, I guess." Rachel goes back to her room on her own. Dr. Shapiro turns to Jeanie. "What do you think? Is Rachel strong enough to handle this situation?"

Jeanie says, "It may be very painful for her, but it may also uncover the demons that contributed to her emotional crash. Often, we see patients after major stress events. Having the opportunity for Dr. Deera to support her before she faces her daughter may be a gift. It may take longer for her to work through her depression if she stays here and doesn't see or talk to her daughter, especially if her daughter dies."

"I agree with you, Jeanie. Let's wait and see how she copes with deciding. Call me as soon as she does."

Jeanie goes back to the nursing station. It was just shy of 30 minutes when Rachel came up to her. "What do you think, Jeanie? What should I do? I kinda want to go, but I'm really scared."

"Rachel, honestly, I think that if you don't go, it will just add to your pile of regrets. This is an opportunity to take a step at getting rid of them instead of adding to them. I also support you in whatever you decide."

Rachel says, "I think you are right. Please ask Dr. Shapiro to make the arrangements. I hope Dr. Deera is as good as you say."

***

David calls home. "Mom, is Dad home yet?"

"He's probably on the way. Is there something wrong?"

"No, there's nothing wrong. Would you call him and ask him if he would stop and pick me up? I have something I would like to do with him."

"OK, I'll give him a call."

"Bye, Mom. See you later."

David returns be with Angela.

Dad knocks on the open door to Angela's room. "Hey, Dad. I'm so glad you got here so soon. Come in and meet Angela, Nana, and Sammy."

"Nice to meet you, Nana, and you too, Sammy." He goes over to Angela and touches her hand. "I'm so glad to finally meet you, Angela. David tells me how special you are to him."

Angela looks him in the eyes to see the Love that he is. Mr. Walden had a surprised look on his face as he gazed into her eyes. They continued this way for almost a whole minute. He didn't know what to say.

David finally interrupted their gaze. "Dad, Angela and I have been talking about giving her oncologist, Dr. Welling, a gift. Angela wondered if I could find the crystal at the park that I dreamed of. It is hidden under a rock. Would you stop on the way home so I could see if it really exists?"

"I think we can do that. We better hurry if we want to find the crystal before it gets dark."

"I'll see you tomorrow, Angela. Love you." David kisses her and rushes out with his dad.

On the way to the park, David's father confesses that meeting Angela was quite an experience. "When I looked into her eyes, I had a surge of energy bursting through my body, followed by goosebumps everywhere. As we continued to look at each other, I felt a profound sense of peace."

"Dad, that's what happens when you become aware that your Loveselves are connected."

They stop at the park, and David leads his dad off the trail through the woods to the stream.

"There are a lot of rocks, David. How can you tell which one hides the crystal?"

"It's the one that will speak to me. Over here, this one." Dad helps David turn over the boulder, and there it is. David picks it up and washes it off.

"OK, we can go home now, Dad. Thanks for bringing me here. I know that you were skeptical about anything being real about my dream."

"I'm not skeptical now."

When they get home, David asks his mom if she could wrap the crystal up as a gift for Angela's doctor. She says she has the perfect box and paper for the crystal.

"Dinner's ready. Let's sit down before it gets cold."

At dinner, Dad relates the story to Mom about finding the crystal. He says he is still a little dumbfounded about how David knew where to find it. "In the past week, I have been bombarded by one mystery after another. I am starting to question my understanding of just about everything. I am surprised that I am not afraid."

Chapter 30

The Perfect Gift

Friday, June 21

Nana stops at David's house to drop off Sammy. Mom answers the door and greets Nana. "Hi Sammy, how are you today?"

"I'm fine," he says with a smile.

"Hey, I see you brought a video game player," says David. "I have one in my room with some games you might like to try."

"Yeah, that would be great."

"Vicki, I am so grateful that you are willing to watch Sammy for me. Babysitters were getting expensive on my limited income. Sammy just didn't want to hang around the hospital today."

"It's my pleasure, Nana. Angela is so much more than a friend to David, and I'm happy to help with anything I can. How is Angela doing?"

"She is comfortable and sleeping more," says Nana. "She focuses on her art when she is awake. I am a little worried because she doesn't want to get out of bed and hasn't been eating much either. I am just in awe and uplifted by David and Angela's profound spiritual connection."

"I asked David if there was anything I could do to help," says Vicki. "He told me to quiet my mind of judgments, open my heart, and focus on the perfection of the Love that I am and the Love that Angela is. He said there was nothing broken, so there is nothing to fix. I'm still confused by how he comes by this information."

"David, are you ready to go to the hospital to visit Angela with me?"

"Yes, this is going to be a very special day. I don't want to miss it."

When Nana and David got to the room, Angela appears to be sleeping. They sat down for only a few minutes before she wakes up. "Good morning, Nana and DavidLove. I wasn't sleeping. I was at the Peace Pond bathing in Love with Roy."

Nana comes over and gives her the first kiss. David gives her the second one and says, "I AM here. I brought you the gift." He hands her the small gift box wrapped in flowered paper and tied with a white ribbon and bow. "Mom wrapped it for me."

"Thanks a lot, DavidLove." She placed it on her tray table, knowing that Dr. Welling would probably be in soon. "Is it alright with you two if I go back to the Peace Pond for a while?"

Nana responds quickly, "Of course, my dear Angela." Nana and David sit in silence until Dr. Welling comes in. David stands up and gives her his chair. She pulls it up to sit near Angela. "How are you doing today, Angela?"

"I am feeling perfectly tired. I just want to sleep and dream."

Dr. Welling says, "I'm so sorry, but I have to tell you, Angela, that the lab tests show us that your cancer is spreading and your organs are shutting down. There isn't anything more we can do for you other than to make you as comfortable as possible." Nana Sage starts to cry, and David reaches for her hand.

"It's okay, Nana. I know I'm dying, and I am not afraid. I have been talking to David and Love about it for the last few days. I am at peace, and I think it is the perfect time to move on to my next adventure. Can we remove the I.V. now?"

Dr. Welling looks over to Nana Sage.

Nana Sage says, "It hurts to give up, but I trust in the wisdom of the Love that Angela is. Yes, you can remove the I.V., Dr. Welling."

"I want to thank you, Dr. Welling, for the wonderful care you have given me. In appreciation, I have a gift for you." She hands the doctor the gift box.

"You didn't have to get me anything."

"I know, but David and I decided this may be the Perfect gift for you at this time. Please open it now. I am excited to see your reaction."

Dr. Welling opens the box and then the tissue paper surrounding the present. Her eyes couldn't have opened any wider when she looked at the crystal. She couldn't hold back her tears. "This means more to me than you could possibly know, Angela. Where did you get it?"

David answers, "When I was in a coma, I had a dream. I was playing The Love Game with God. I was in the park, letting joy guide me to where I might actually see God. I veered off the trail and came to a stream. I looked around for a while until I saw a boulder that spoke to me: 'David, turn me over.' This is what I found. The gem introduced herself to me as Crystal. Crystal helped me see Love that day. In my dream, I took Crystal home with me and kept it close to me every day."

"If it was a dream, how did you get this crystal?"

Angela responds, "David and I talked yesterday about giving you a gift. I had a feeling that this might mean something special to you. David asked his dad to take him to the park yesterday to the place where Crystal was resting. He turned over the boulder, and there it was, just as he dreamed. David's mom helped him with the gift wrapping, and he brought it to me today."

"This story blows my mind. Would you like to know why this is such a special gift to me, Angela?"

"Yes, yes, I do," says Angela.

"Me too," David adds.

"Do you know my first name, Angela?"

"No, I don't."

"It's Crystal. Let me tell you a story about this particular Crystal. I recognized this unique gem right away when I saw it. My dad gave it to me as a child. He had found it when he was a young boy in a stream in the woods by the park. He loved the crystal, and that's where my name came from. He died of cancer when I was 14 years old. I was devastated by his death and had intended to bury the crystal with him in his casket so that his spirit would not feel alone. I was even more distraught at the funeral when I realized that I had left Crystal at home. I was resistant to giving her up for a while after that. I saw it as a symbol of my dad's love. Eventually, I decided to offer the crystal back to the earth as a symbol of my love for my dad. I took it back to the area near where my dad said he found it and buried it under a big rock in the stream. That was 30 years ago. I became an oncologist to honor him.

Angela says, "It is no accident that it has come back to you. Maybe you can pass it on to your son, who never had the chance to know your dad. That way, he might find the love in it that your dad saw. Again, thank you so much, Crystal, for your care."

She and Angela hug, tears flowing down both their cheeks. Then Crystal looks into Angela's eyes and says, "I see the love you are, and I feel perfect." She then turns to look into David's eyes and sees the same thing. "I see the love you are, and I feel perfect. I can't express how much appreciation I have for you for retrieving this gem for me. Nana Sage, my life has been so enriched by Angela. I'm so sorry I couldn't do more."

Dr. Welling holds Crystal to her chest with one hand and wipes her tears away with the other as she walks out.

Angela looks at Nana and David and says, "Wasn't that a magnificent Love experience? This part of the Love story of my life may be coming to a close, but love tells me my

Loveself keeps living after it leaves this body. It is so comforting to know that both of you will be with me when I make the transition. I'm heading back to the Peace Pond. I'm really happy."

A knock on the door breaks the silence that had filled the room for the past hour. The door slowly opens to reveal Mrs. Deera. "How's my two Love Game dream buddies," she asks?

David jumps up to hug her, and Angela blurts out an enthusiastic, "Yes!" "Nana, this is Mrs. Deera, Dr. Deera's mother, who we have been talking about."

"I'm Nana. So glad to meet you, Mrs. Deera."

"You can call me Amma. It's nice to meet you too. So, how is everyone doing?"

Angela says, "I've been feeling perfect this morning sitting by the Peace Pond."

David says, "I've been feeling perfect being near Angela and Nana."

Nana follows with, "I've been a little sad that Angela's doctor said there was nothing more they could do for her and her organs are shutting down."

"I'm sorry to hear that, Nana. Angela, you must really be connected to your Loveself if you are still feeling perfect after hearing the news. Are you afraid?"

"I'm now open to my Loveself, but earlier last week, before I met David Love, I was afraid. I have moments of fear, Mrs. Deera, but they quickly disappear into the Peace Pond. What I do experience more often is curiosity about my new adventure. However, Love reminds me to keep creating and living my Love story moment by moment. Do you know what heaven is, Mrs. Deera? It is the 'Perfect Now' that I am experiencing. I see Love everywhere."

"Thank you, Angela. I'm sharing heaven with you. I have come today with an open heart and a bag of freshly baked chocolate chip cookies. Anyone want one?"

David and Angela simultaneously raise their hands and say, "I do."

Mrs. Deera laughs and says, "Your 'I do's' sound like you're getting married."

David and Angela again respond in unison, "We are."

Nana said, "You two don't need to get married; you are already united."

Mrs. Deera nods with a smile. Although she hasn't had any food lately, Angela nibbles on a cookie followed by a sip of water. "Thank you for being so kind."

"You're welcome, Angela. You will always have a home in my heart."

David devours his cookie. "Can I have one more, Mrs. Deera?"

"Sure, David. I'll leave the bag for you guys. You might save one for my son if he shows up."

"Oh, by the way, since I haven't dreamed with you in the last week, I was wondering if you knew about Roy passing. I found out last Friday night that he had passed earlier in the day before we were together at the Peace Pond. I remember him saying he was in heaven, but I thought he meant heaven on earth."

Angela said, "Dr. Deera told us the other day about Roy. I saw him again earlier today when I was at the Peace Pond. He told me his experience with death was wonderful and that he would be present for me when I passed from this physical life."

Mrs. Deera says, "I'm glad Roy has found a new purpose in service to Love. I'm going to leave now, knowing all is perfectly well." She gives Angela a kiss and a hug, then a kiss and a hug for David. She hugs Nana and whispers in her ear, "I see the Love you are too."

"I AM here."

A chorus of "Yes's" fills the room.

Angela calls out to Mrs. Deera as she walks out the door, "See you later, alligator."

Mrs. Deera turns and says with a smile, "In a while, crocodile."

Chapter 31

Rachel Visits

Dr. Deera enters Angela's room.

"Good day to you all. How are you, Angela?"

"Dreamy, Dr. Deera. I was happy that your mom stopped by to see me earlier. She left a chocolate chip cookie for you."

"That was nice of her. Nana, can I buy you a cup of coffee? I'll take a cookie with me. I would like to talk to you. Are you kids OK for a while?"

They nod their heads.

Nana and Dr. Deera sit down in the coffee shop. "What's up, Dr. Deera?"

"I wanted to let you know that Rachel is being transferred to our Behavioral Wellness Unit this morning. I am going to see if I can help her reunite with Angela. I was hoping to get some background information from your perspective before I meet with her. Would that be okay?"

"I am so happy about the possibility that Rachel and Angela can see each other before Angela dies. What would you like to know?"

"I'll leave it up to you to relate anything about Rachel that you feel might help."

"My husband, William, had a great job. We had a comfortable life. Rachel and her dad had a very close relationship. She idolized him. Our lives were turned upside down when William was killed in a car accident. The driver of a semi-truck fell asleep at the wheel. His truck swerved, knocking William off the road and into a tree. Rachel was 13 at the time and was devastated. I was so consumed with my own grief that I wasn't much of a support for her. Rachel started acting out, hanging around with some troubled kids. Her grades plummeted, and we always fought about something. We eventually got a settlement from the trucking company as well as a life insurance payment. That has been supporting us."

"Rachel left home soon after finishing high school. I lost contact with her for two years. She showed up at my door pregnant and wanted a place to stay. She couldn't work at that late stage in her pregnancy. I asked if the father of the baby could help. She told me she didn't know who the father was. She had been with so many men she couldn't tell. Well, of course, I took her in. When Angela was born, the doctors did a lot of testing to make sure she was OK. That's when I found out Rachel had been on street drugs during her pregnancy. Thank God Angela was healthy. She went into rehab after the birth and was well for a while. She thought she had found the love of her life with a musician she met in rehab. He was moving to another city and wanted her to follow him. He told her that Angela could come along. I was heartbroken when Angela left. I had become very close to her."

Nana took a breath and continued. It wasn't long after they moved away that Rachel's boyfriend dumped her for another woman. She tried to raise Angela on her own, and I think she was selling herself to survive. She got pregnant with Sammy but again wasn't sure who his father was. Complications after Sammy's birth required surgery that prevented her from ever getting pregnant again. She was determined to care for her kids. She worked full-time as a waitress in a nice restaurant and part-time for a catering company. She had friends with children who cared for the kids while she was at work. Everything seemed to be going well until Angela was diagnosed with cancer. Rachel lost control and started drinking alcohol heavily. She was fired from her job. I think she couldn't handle the thought of Angela dying and leaving her like her father did."

"The State Department of Child Safety threatened to take the kids away from her after receiving complaints that she was leaving the children alone. I was more than happy to take them. Rachel's depression worsened, and about six weeks ago, she was admitted to the hospital. We haven't had any contact since she was hospitalized. I hope this helps, Dr. Deera."

"Thank you so much. What you told me is very helpful. I'll see you later, hopefully with Rachel."

Rachel is transferred to Wellco's behavioral health unit and gets settled in her room. It's about noon when Dr. Deera meets with her. They discuss her depression and her apprehension about meeting with Angela. He calls his secretary to ask her to reschedule his appointments for the afternoon. Rachel is trembling as she and Dr. Deera wait for the elevator.

"You're not alone, Rachel. You can change your mind at any time. Let's just take one step at a time to reunite with Angela."

Dr. Deera tells her know that Nana and Angela's friend David will also be present.

Rachel gets to the door, sees Angela, and then retreats. "I can't do this, Dr. Deera; please take me back.

Angela starts crying. Nana rushes to her side to comfort her, and David bolts out of the room. Dr. Deera is guiding Rachel back to the psych unit when he hears David.

"Dr. Deera, Dr. Deera, please stop for a moment."

Dr. Deera and Rachel stop and turn toward David. "Please, Dr. Deera, can I speak to Rachel? I will only take only a couple moments of your time.

Dr. Deera looks at Rachel for approval. Rachel asks, "who are you?"

"I'm David, and I'm Angela's best friend." Rachel nods her approval to Dr. Deera. They step to the side of the hall, away from the nurse's station.

David looks directly into Rachel's eyes. "I see the real you, Rachel. I see through all the shit stories that have covered your heart. And what I see is the effect Love that you are. I see that light within you trying to burst into the world. Now, here's the thing. I know without any doubt whatsoever that Angela will see the same thing. She is in such a state of Love, I mean, she is Love, right now, and she sees and appreciates perfection in everything. You don't need to say or do anything; just be at her bedside. You will experience Love like you've never known when you look into her eyes. The Light from her Loveself will penetrate your whole being and free you from the prison you have been living in. Rachel, please give Love a chance."

Rachel looks to Dr. Deera, whose eyes are watering, and says, "I can't describe what I'm feeling, but it's not fear. I want to give Love a chance." Dr. Deera puts his hand on David's shoulder and whispers to him, "Are you vying for my job?" David smiles and reaches for Rachel's hand as they walk back to Angela's room.

Rachel goes in and sees bald little Angela, and she starts crying. Oh, Momma, come here next to me; I miss you so much. Nana steps away as Rachel gets close to Angela. When Rachel looks into Angela's eyes, as David had said, her tears stop, and she is overwhelmed by a feeling that radiates through her body. She appears to be momentarily paralyzed, her wide eyes staring into space.

"What's happening, Momma?"

"I don't know, my baby. There is electricity pulsing through my body, mixing feelings of joy, calm excitement, peace, massive appreciation, and a sense of deep connection to everything. The only word that floats to the surface is 'perfect.' I see the Love you are, and I feel Perfect."

Angela says, "That is Divine Love, Momma. I'll share a little secret with you. The perfect Love you recognize in me is but a reflection of the Love that radiates from your own open heart."

Nana comes over next to Rachel. "May I have a hug, Rachel?"

"Oh, yes, Momma. I would love to feel your touch again. I have felt so disconnected from everything important to me."

After watching them hug for a while, Angela says, "You know I like hugs too." Angela sits up to receive a threesome hug.

Dr. Deera watches the miracle before him, and all he says is, "Wow! Wow! -- Wow!"

David turns to him and says, "That's perfection." He then extends his arms to Dr. Deera, looks him in the eyes, and says, "You want some?"

Dr. Deera says, "Yes, I do, David. Yes, I do."

As they hug, David whispers to him, "You already have it."

Dr. Deera says, "I would like to leave you guys alone. I will be back in a while."

"Please, Dr. Deera, don't leave. I think it is important that you stay. You have had a valuable role in David's and my Love story. And you will continue to. Love tells me that you will also help Momma and Nana to write their own Love stories."

"I am honored to be included, Angela."

"Momma, You know I'm dying. Love says that I'm going to leave this body, but my LoveSelf, that part of me you saw when you looked into my eyes, will live on within your heart. I am so glad that you have been my Momma, and I will always be here as Love for you."

Tears rolled down Rachel's cheeks. "I'm so sorry that I abandoned you when you needed me. I can't forgive myself. I wanted to make it up to you, but if you die, I won't have the chance."

"Momma, there is nothing to forgive. Love tells me that everyone is trying to care for themselves the best they can in each moment, and most importantly, each moment is perfect. It couldn't be any other way than the way it is. The beauty of Love is that we have been blessed with the gift of choosing a different way of caring for ourselves the next moment. We can change the focus of our attention and make ourselves happy. I am happy, Momma. Do you hear me? I am really happy! I imagine that when you first looked into my eyes for the first time when I was born, you might have wished that I would have a happy life. Well, your dream came true."

Angela is on a roll now. She continues: "Everything that happened in this life and all my lives before has led me to this perfect moment of Love. Everything that you have done for me and have not done for me has been a gift. That is why you don't need forgiveness. Momma, I see the Love that you are, and I feel perfect. Look into my eyes, and you will know that everything I tell you is the truth of Love. I will always be your Angel."

With tears welling in her eyes, Rachel tenderly tells her daughter, "What you have just shared is a more cherished gift than I could ever imagine. It is a gift that, up until this moment, I would have rejected because I didn't believe I was worthy of Love. You have opened my heart to a feeling of perfection that I thought was impossible."

David walks up and takes Angela's hand. Angela says, "David and I have another gift for you, Momma, and you too, Dr. Deera. It is the Love Game we have been playing in the last couple of weeks. There are two games you can play in Life. Everyone is familiar with the survival game. This is a competitive game focused on self-preservation, rooted in the notion of being separate from others, other creatures, the environment, and Divine Love. This game operates on the principle that all our desires, such as Love, security, health, worthiness, and wealth, come from outside ourselves. What makes it challenging is the premise that there is a limited amount of whatever you want, so you must take control, work tirelessly, and even fight to get what you want. This past and future-oriented game is dependent on judgments. Heaven is possible only after we die; until then, nothing is perfect.

David then says, "The other game that we can play is the Love Game. In this game, we look for Love, the Source, the Oneness, the God that connects us all and is always present everywhere. The only thing that keeps us from experiencing Divine Love is our beliefs, judgments, and fears. Love says there is enough of everything anyone could desire. Everyone and every situation is perfect. Nothing is lacking; you don't have to struggle or fight to get it. In this game, Love asks us to create our own Love story by listening to the voice of our hearts and keeping our eyes open to possibilities found in the present moment. Love reminds us that we all have the power to make ourselves happy regardless of the situation, but only in the present moment and never in the future. If you want something in the future, make yourself happy now.

Angela follows, "There are three levels of the game, each one more challenging. The first level is finding love in beings that we like and appreciate. The second level is finding Love in those we dislike or fear, including ourselves. And the third level challenges us to find Love within difficult situations beyond our control. The lesson here is that the Love we seek at every level isn't about the object of our focus as much as it is about opening our hearts to The Love that we already embody and letting it shine on what we see. I am happy."

David says, "There you have it. May your life be as enriched playing this game as it has been for us."

"Nana, can you come close to me?" Nana goes to Angela and holds her hand. They look deeply into each other's eyes. Tears flood Nana's eyes. "I don't know if I have told you enough, Nana, how much you mean to me. I see you as perfect Love—an essential part of The Love Story of My Life. I will forever be grateful to you for being here for me. My Love story doesn't end with my death, Nana. I will always be here for you. Like playing the Love Game, 'if you listen with your heart and keep your eyes open, you will see Me. Also, don't be surprised if I show up in your dreams."

"My dear, dear Angela, you are such a precious gift to me. You have shown this old dog new tricks -- the way I see my life, the world, and Love. You have transformed my life and shown me it's possible to be Love in the flesh."

Nana gives Angela a kiss and a hug. "Yes, I will see you in the morning.

David then goes up to Angela, squeezes her hand, leans over, gently touches her cheek, and kisses her dry lips. He gazes into her eyes, communicating what words couldn't. He turns away, leaving her smiling, and then leaves with Nana.

Rachel and Dr. Deera stay with Angela the rest of the afternoon while Angela goes in and out of her dream states.

Nana drives David home to pick up Sammy.

Mom says, "Hi, Nana. We are still about ready to eat, and I've already set a place for you. We're having spaghetti tonight."

"Thank you so much, Vicki. That sounds really good. I've had a really emotional day. I don't know how much longer it will be before Angela dies. It could be tonight or in a few days. She hasn't eaten or drunk anything for a while now. I want to be there with her, but I also want to be with Sammy. I feel I've been away from him so much. Angela told me she didn't need me by her bedside because she was with Love."

Dad said grace and added a plea for God to be with Angela.

David smiled; accepting the plea was important for Dad but not necessary for Angela.

Dinner was tranquil.

After dinner, Mom started clearing the table. Nana jumped up and said, "let me help you, Vicki."

Michael and David also stood up to help. Mom signaled them to sit down. "You guys can have the night off. Your dad is going to help me."

"Oh, I guess I am," says Dad.

Both boys responded enthusiastically, "All Right!"

Mom and Nana took the dishes into the kitchen. Nana continues, "You have been so kind to me; I can't thank you enough for taking care of Sammy."

Dad finishes clearing the table and joins Nana and Mom in the kitchen.

Nana says, "I want to thank you for allowing David to be at the hospital these last few days. I realize the enormity of stress you must have experienced when he was in a coma. I suspect it was hard not having him around you all the time after he was discharged from the hospital. But his presence with Angela has lifted much weight off my shoulders. I wasn't always sure of what to say or how to be a comfort to

208

her. Witnessing the way they interacted with each other taught me what Love is all about.

Nana says to Sammy, "It's time to go home. Get your video game player."

David gives Nana a goodbye hug. "I'm going up to my room to dream with Angela. See you tomorrow."

"Yes, see you tomorrow."

David lays down on his bed and quickly finds himself next to Angela. I knew you would come to be with me, DavidLove. He gets into bed with her and holds her as they fall asleep. "I AM here."

Chapter 32

Celebration

Saturday, June 22

"Wake up, kids, it's time to play."

David wakes up with Angela. They look out the window. It's still dark.

Angela says, "I think it's time for me to leave this body. Let's invite Nana, Momma, Sammy, Dr. and Mrs. Deera, and Dr. Welling to join us at the Peace Pond. Roy says he's already there for us."

"Love, can you help us wake them up to be with us?"

"Of course, I can. Love Ones."

"Angela and David take themselves to the Peace Pond and wait as Rachel, Nana, and Sammy appear. Rachel and Sammy give each other a long hug before they hold hands to form a circle with the others. The life force energy was felt moving through one arm, passing through the heart, and out the other arm into the next person. The full moon's light reflected on the lake as if it were midday. They notice that Dr. Deera, his mother, and Dr. Welling were standing back and watching this celebration. Angela calls to them to join in the circle. Nana and David dropped their hands to let the three others join in between them.

"Thanks for coming to be with me in celebration of my passing into a new reality. I have invited a few more friends, who you may recognize, to be with me on my journey. Behind her, hovering over the pond, were images of Roy, William, Robert, Maggie, Mary, and Crystal's father." Everyone had the perfect feeling as they looked up in awe at the beautiful spirits. Angela says, "Now, Love Ones, silently, take a few moments and look into the eyes of each person here, then listen to what your heart has to say." After everyone had the opportunity to look into each other's eyes, they heard a voice say, "I AM here. Do you see me now?"

"Angela says, "That is Divine Love speaking, my friends. You have just heard the voice of God and seen Love in the hearts of everyone in this circle. Remember, Divine Love is present as your Loveself. Now my Loveself tells me I have done what I needed to as a human. It says it's time to move out of this body and into my new role as an angel. Our Love stories will continue to be written together. My dream is that you listen with the ears of your heart, see the perfection in each moment, free your Divine Loveself, and celebrate the eternal Love Story we are creating as One."

Angela closes her eyes, breaks the circle, and walks into the pond. Still holding hands, witnesses string out along the bank, watching Angela wade deeper into the pond until she disappears. They stare into the stillness. A concentric ripple appears on the surface, and a radiant image of Angela emerges.

"Let's reconnect the circle," says David. As they stand again in the circle, Angela's radiant image moves from the pond to hover just above the circle. An energy surges through their arms and hearts, each one experiencing the perfect feeling of Love's presence. As they appreciate the beauty of Angela's transformation, the Heavenly Being clones herself into seven images that descend to eye level. Then, each person has their own Divine image of Angela flying into their open heart.

212

Angela's image rises to join the other Spirit friends before fading into the night sky. There were no tears, only serene smiles, knowing that all was well. The circle broke up, with everyone sharing hugs. Time seemed to stop until they found themselves back in bed.

Caroline, the night nurse, heard Angela's help call signal, looked at the clock, and saw it was 2:22 am. She went to check on her. Initially, she thought Angela was sleeping. She was stumped as to how the help call button got pushed. It was out of Angela's reach. When she noticed Angela was not breathing, she confirmed the absence of a carotid pulse. She took a third step and listened with a stethoscope to Angela's heart. Caroline was sad to think another innocent young soul moved on without the chance to experience a full life. There was a DNR sign on the door, so she didn't call for a resuscitation team, but she did call one of the resident doctors to come and pronounce Angela's death. It was especially difficult for Caroline to notify the family if they hadn't been present. She calls Nana Sage's number. Nana Sage answers. "Nana Sage?"

"Yes,"

"This is Caroline, the night charge nurse at Wellco General."

Nana says, "I was expecting your call about Angela's passing. To save you the awkwardness, I already know. I was with Angela when she died."

"You were here?"

"No, I was with Angela at the Peace Pond."

"What? Angela is here. I'm confused. How could Angela be in two places at once?"

"It was a dream, Caroline."

Caroline said, "Dreaming that you were with Angela's death might explain how you knew, but it doesn't make sense how the call button got pushed."

"It's a mystery, Caroline. Maybe you were dreaming, too. Anyway, I have already made arrangements with the Berd and Liten Funeral Home. You can call them to pick up Angela.

Thanks for calling."

Caroline hangs up, takes a deep breath, then lets it out with an "uh." She rubs her neck. The furrowed brow and narrowed eyes staring down reflect her inner conflict. She then puts her confusion aside and calls the funeral home. There was a note on Angela's chart to call Dr. Welling day or night when she passed. She called Dr. Welling, "Dr. Welling, sorry to bother you. This is Caroline, the pediatric unit charge nurse. I have a note on Angela's chart that you wanted to be called when she passed. Angela died a little while ago."

"Thanks for calling Caroline, but I am aware that she died."

"I talked to Nana Sage, and she said you were with Angela and the others at the Peace Pond. Is that how you knew?"

Dr. Welling said, "Yes, Caroline, we are all sharing a dream. Angela and David have been doing it for the last couple of weeks. I think Nana Sage and Sammy just joined in recently."

"But Dr. Welling, dreams can't make things happen. How did Angela's call button get pushed, alerting me to check on her? "

"Dreams make things happen all the time. There are so many unexplainable things happening out there, and most of the time, it's easier to dismiss them rather than just accept them. I have witnessed firsthand the mystery of David and Angela's relationship and how they have touched the people around them. It's mind-boggling and beyond any scientific explanation. Thanks for calling, Caroline, and have a good night."

Another call light goes on, diverting her attention from the craziness Caroline is experiencing.

At 7:00 am, Dr. Deera gets a call from the secretary of the psych unit. "Did you hear that Angela died in the middle of the night?"

"I am aware she died."

"I don't think Rachel knows yet; she hasn't come out of her room yet. Do you want the nurse to tell her when she does?"

"No, It's not necessary. Rachel knows. She was with Angela when she died. When she gets up, let her know I'm on my way in and that I would like to talk to her about the beautiful experience we shared."

The unit secretary turns to the nurse and relays the strange message that Dr. Deera has told her.

The nurse says, "Angela hasn't left her room all night. How could she know about Angela, and how could Dr. Deera and Rachel experience anything together last night? This doesn't make sense. Maybe I've worked in this unit too long, and it's time for me to move on?"

Dr. Deera arrives wearing khakis and a flowered shirt. The nurse and unit secretary look at each other in disbelief. They had never seen Dr. Deera wear anything so casual and, especially, without his signature white lab coat. Rachel is sitting in the common area, smiling. She has an unexpected sparkle in her eyes.

"Hi, Dr. Deera. Isn't it a great day?"

Dr. Deera sits down beside Rachel. "Yes, it is. I feel so blessed to have been included in the beautiful ceremony we shared last night. I can feel Angela in my heart at this very moment."

"I do, too. I thought I might feel more pain in my heart when she passed, but the opposite occurred. It was so amazing. I had that Perfect experience of Love's presence again. Yesterday, she taught us to play the Love Game. I have been so consumed by playing Survival games all my life that I didn't know there was another choice.

"Rachel, how do you feel about going home today to be with your mother and Sammy? Do you have any urge to have a drink of alcohol or to hurt yourself?"

"You know, I haven't thought about it once since reuniting with Angela. I realize that I need to abstain one day at a time. I think I have resources that I can turn to now that I've never had before."

"Rachel, I feel confident that you are ready to break out of here. I have seen a miraculous change in you, and your life will never be the same. I see the Love that you are and I also feel perfect. You are and will continue to be a gift to all."

"Dr. Deera, thank you so much for your support. Yes, I would really like to go home."

"My secretary will call you to set up a follow-up appointment in a week. The charge nurse will take care of your discharge and give you prescriptions that I recommend you continue. We will talk about whether you need them long-term when I see you again. You know how the experiences in the last few days have transformed your life, and they have also had a major impact on my life. I, too, have started playing the Love Game. Okay, If I give you a hug?"

"Absolutely."

The secretary's jaw drops as she looks over at Dr. Deera and Rachel hugging. She asks the charge nurse, "Have you ever seen Dr. Deera hug anyone before? What's got into him? I think that's against the rules."

"I don't know, but I think it's kind of nice that he has loosened up a bit."

With eyes beaming, Rachel dances over to the nurse's station desk and says, "I'm going home!"

The nurse says, "I'm sorry for your loss, Rachel."

"Thank you so much for your care," says Rachel. She points to her heart and says, "My Angel is right here."

Dr. Deera picks up his cell phone and calls Dr. Welling. "Good morning, Crystal; this is Mark. I'll get right to the point. May I take you to dinner tonight?"

"You mean like a date?"

"Yes. A date. I have been meaning to ask you for a while, but the events last night convinced me not to wait any longer. What do you say?"

"Mark, I felt we had a connection when we first met, but our lives never aligned until this past week. I hoped you would ask me out, and if you hadn't soon, I was going to make the first move."

"What time would you like me to pick you up?"

"How about 7?"

"Great, I will see you then." Dr. Deera hung up, pumped his fist, and said, "Hot, damn!"

He goes to the nurses' station to make a note on Rachel's chart, writes her prescriptions, and orders her discharge. He told the nurse that he was available for emergencies only today. The resident doctor will check in with the patients

216

and handle non-emergencies. "I'm going to spend the day with my mom. You all have a lovely day."

***

David wakes up later than usual and goes down for breakfast. "Hey, Mom."

"Good morning, David. Did you sleep well?"

"I'm a little tired. I was up with Angela last night. I was present when she died."

"She died? Honey, I'm so sorry. I know how close you two were. What do you mean you were there?"

"Love woke Angela and me up. Angela said it was time to leave her body, and she asked Love to invite Nana, Rachel, Sammy, Dr. Deera, his mom, and Dr. Welling to meet us at the Peace Pond. Roy was already there. We were all holding hands when Angela let us go and disappeared into the peace pond. It was very beautiful. We saw her emerge as a radiant Angel. She hovered in the middle of our circle, and then she cloned seven of her Loveselves. One clone flew into each of our open hearts. It was a celebration of a Perfect life. No sadness, just that Perfect feeling of Love. Angela's last words serve as a profound reminder of how I want to live my life." She said, "My dream is that you listen with the ears of your heart, see the perfection in each moment, free your Divine Loveself, and celebrate the eternal Love Story we are creating together as One."

"Wow, David. For me, those are inspirational words that evoke a deep emotional truth to their wisdom."

"I agree."

***

Nana Sage answers the knock at her door. Her eyes light up when she sees Rachel. "Welcome home, baby. Come on in. I'm so glad you were able to get out of the hospital to be with me and Sammy."

"It's great to be home, Momma. Yes, Dr. Deera felt confident that I was going to be fine. Where's Sammy?" Sammy heard his mother's voice and came running. "Momma, Momma, you're back."

She hugs and kisses him. "I'm never going to leave you again."

"Rachel, come into the kitchen while Sammy finishes his lunch. You want some coffee? I have a fresh pot already made. Are you hungry?"

"Yes, momma, I'll take some coffee, but I'm not hungry right now." Rachel holds Sammy close to her and shuffle to the kitchen. Sammy sits down and with eyes glued on Rachel, takes another bite of his peanut butter and jelly sandwich. Nana and Rachel sit down next to each other at the table. They gaze into each other's eyes silently communicating their incredible experience.

Chapter 33

Rooting for Butch

Sunday, June 23

"Wake up, DavidLove, it's time to play."

"Angela, is that you?"

"Yes, it is. I wanted to be the one to wake you today and join you in your games."

"That would be perfect. What's being an angel like for you?"

"Like that wonderful Perfect feeling we had, but now it's all the time. It's like laughing without a body. Love gave me a choice to be in a state of being that allows me to support incarnated souls on their journey or reincarnate into another physical life. Our love story is still in progress. I choose to be here for you. What do you say? Would you like to play your games with me today, DavidLove?"

"Absolutely. I'm thinking about going back to Sunday School this morning. I would like to tell Mr. Rigid that I have seen and talked with Love."

"You could plan to do that, David Love, or you could just wait and see what the moment brings."

"When I hear you talk, Angela, my heart feels like it is too big to fit into my chest. You help bring out that perfect part of me.

David went down for breakfast. Michael and Tom are already sitting at the table.

Mom greets David. "Good morning, honey, how did you sleep last night?

"I slept well and was surprised to have Angela wake me up this morning. She chose to stay in a state of being that allowed her to help me finish our Love story. I know Love is always present, but I enjoy remembering Angela as Love."

"I guess that makes Angela your Angel. What a gift, David," Mom says.

David smiles. "Yes, she is my Angel Love!"

"Here are your Cheerios. Would you like me to put sliced bananas on it?"

"That would be nice, Mom."

"You were dreaming again," proclaimed Michael. "You didn't really talk with a dead person."

"Yes, I did as clear as I'm talking to you right now and by the way, I was wide awake."

Michael rolled his eyes, "Yeah, I'm sure you were."

"If you would open your heart, you might also talk with souls in the spirit world, Michael."

"I can't imagine why I would possibly want to."

"Well, Michael, I see the Love that you are. I know that someday, when you are ready, you will look into your heart and see the perfect Love that you are, too."

Without another response, Michael finishes eating his cereal and toast.

Mom brings some toast slices, already jellied, to David. "How do you feel about going back to Sunday school today?"

"I thought I might go back. Angela invited me not to think about it too far ahead of time and to let the moment arise as it is. I am open to the possibility of going. These Cheerios taste really good. Thanks for adding the bananas."

Dad comes in and sits next to David. He sips his coffee and tells Mom that he only wants a sweet roll this morning. "How are you feeling this morning, David?"

"I'm feeling great. Angela woke me up this morning to play my games with me."

Mom interjects, "Angela has been his angel since she died."

Dad says, "I'm sorry she died, but I think it's wonderful that the Love she is still communicates with you."

"You've changed in the last two weeks, Dad. I don't think you would have liked hearing me tell you that someone who is dead talks to me. I am so appreciative of the way you supported me without judgment when I wanted to find the Crystal."

"You're right about that. The last couple of weeks of chaotic emotional experiences have challenged my beliefs about what is and is not possible. Do you want to go to Sunday School today?"

"Thanks for asking, Dad."

"Yes, I want to go. Love reminds me that every experience has value, including Sunday School. Every situation gives me the opportunity to show up as Love or not. Not that it really matters, but I'm curious to see if Mr. Rigid notices any change in me since my experiences with Love."

"Sounds like fun, David."

David runs upstairs to get his Sunday clothes on and gets back just as Dad finishes eating. "OK, boys, let's go."

"Dad, would you stop by Nana Sage's house after church? I want to tell her that I've been dreaming with Angela again."

"We can make that happen." Dad says to Mom, "We are going to be a little late for lunch. I'll give you a call when we are leaving Nana Sage's house.

David enters the Sunday school class and heads for his favorite chair. Instead of turning the chair to the window, he decides to move it closer to the other kids, "Hi, everyone." He was surprised when Jeremy said, "Hi David, nice to have you back." The other kids followed with their greetings.

"Wow," David thought and smiled, "I'm glad to be back."

Jeremy says, "Heard you got sick after the last time you were here. Someone called our parents the next day and told us we had to get tested to make sure we didn't get what you had. How are you feeling now?"

"I'm feeling great now, thanks. Even though I had an infection, it is all gone now, and you can't get it."

Mr. Rigid entered the classroom. "Good morning, class, and nice to see you back, David."

David chose to play the Love game and focus on the moment, seeing each person in the room as Love. It didn't matter what stories they were telling. It mattered that each one was caring for themselves. David imagined Mr. Rigid's purpose was to share his perspectives and understanding of the Bible as a way to serve others and to make a difference in their lives. The stories he tells himself fulfill some emotional or spiritual need. He imagined Mr. Rigid as an 11-year-old like him and Angela, trying to find meaning and sense of the struggles in his life. David didn't challenge Mr. Rigid's stories. He also didn't need to change Mr. Rigid's beliefs to align with what Love taught him.

After the class was over, Mr. Rigid came up to David. "How did you feel about the class today? It seemed you were more focused on what I was saying today than in the past."

David said, "Yes, I was more focused. It was a perfect class."

"Perfect?" Mr. Rigid said with eyebrows raised.

"Yes, perfect? We can talk more about that at another time if you're curious. Bye now, see you next week." David turns away and heads to meet Dad for the church service.

Dad catches David before going into the sanctuary and says, "Let's skip church today and worship Love in the park. We can stop and see Nana Sage." David hugs his dad and they go out the back door to the parking lot.

Michael was already waiting in the car. "What's going on, Dad?"

"We're going to make a couple of stops on the way home, Michael. Alright with you?"

"Yeah, Dad, Okay. I didn't really feel like sitting inside today."

"I can't wait to show you where I met Angela," says David.

At the park, David starts running. Dad says, "Slow down, I'm coming."

"This is it." David sits on the bench as Dad and Michael catch up.

The three of them sit together, appreciating the natural surroundings.

"I AM here."

"What was that?" Michael asks as he looks around for the source. Dad's eyes open wide with eyebrows raised."

Before David could tell them that it was Love's presence, Chickadee flew down and landed on his hand.

"Hi, Chickadee. I'm here with my dad and brother. How are you doing today?"

"I was just having fun flying with Angela. Nice to see you here."

David tells Dad and Michael, "Chickadee was the one who reminded me that God and Love were one and the same. Angela also saw Love for the first time when we were with Chickadee. Chickadee jumps on David's shoulder and looks straight into Dad's eyes.

Dad's mouth dropped open.

"I AM here."

"That's Love speaking."

Chickadee then jumps on Dad's shoulder to look into Michael's eyes.

"I have never seen anything so beautiful," says Michael. "I feel so blessed to be here. Thank you, Chickadee." He turns to Dad and says, "I don't remember feeling such joy before."

"May you guys enjoy a 'Loveful' day," says Chickadee as she flies off.

The three sit in silent reverence, reflecting on their Chickadee experience.

David says, "Amen. Let's go see Nana now."

On the way to Nana's house, Michael comments that he is still bewildered over what happened at the park. Dad says, "Maybe it's a good thing to have our beliefs of what is possible shaken up periodically."

David offers, "Maybe it would be helpful to ease our grip on any judgment in order to know the freedom found in Love."

"You sound like an old person, David."

"Well, thank you, Michael."

David rings the doorbell and is surprised to see Rachel open the door.

"Please come in, David."

David says, "I am so glad you are home, Rachel. This is my dad and older brother Michael."

He opens his arms toward her, and she responds with a warm hug.

She turns to Dad and Michael, "Would you like some coffee or tea."

"We can't stay long," Dad says. "Vicki has lunch waiting for us at home. We were wondering how you and Nana are doing and if we can do anything to help."

"I am doing better than I have for a very long time. I will continue to get support from Dr. Deera. Playing the Love Game that Angela and David taught us will greatly help my recovery."

Nana walks in and says, "Hi, I'm so glad you all stopped by." She gives David a hug and a kiss on his cheek.

"I wanted to tell you that Angela woke me up today to play," David says. "I asked her about what it was like where she was. She said it felt perfect, like laughing without a body. We are going to continue dreaming together. Dad, Michael, and I were just at the park and sat on the bench where I first met Angela. Chickadee came and told us she had just been flying with Angela. How great is that?"

"That is wonderful, David. Thank you so much for being a part of our family.

Rachel raises her hand. "I second that."

David crosses his hands over his heart, opens them, palms up, and extends them toward Rachel and Nana. "I see the Love you both are, and I feel perfect. Bye for now Love Ones."

"Let's go, Dad."

Nana walks them over to the door. "I know we will be seeing more of each other. Bye."

***

David runs into the house first followed by his dad and Michael. "Hey guys," says Mom, "Lunch is ready for you. I'm so excited to hear how it went at church today."

In between bites, Dad relates the events of the morning.

"I can't believe you played hooky at church. You've never done that before."

"You didn't know I was a wild and crazy guy," Dad says.

Michael and David both snickered. Michael rolled his eyes, smiled, and said, "Yes, he is a really wild and crazy guy."

"I wasn't really playing hooky. We went to church in the park."

"Oh, Okay then," mom replied with a smirk.

After lunch, David changes his clothes and tells Mom, I'm going down the street to watch the guys play ball. "I'll be back in a while."

The game is in process when David gets there. Butch speaks up, "What are you doing here? I thought you were sick or something."

"I was sick but better now. I came to watch you guys play. I figure that even if I can't play, I can still enjoy watching you guys. Okay?"

David takes a seat on a log by the field and cheers for everyone to do well.

When Butch comes up to bat, David screams, "hit the ball out of the park." Butch turns this head toward David and offers a slight nod and a thankful grin. Two pitches later, he hit the ball in the backyard of the neighboring house. Butch rounds the bases and sees David clapping and then giving some black girl a high five.

Epilogue

Sunday, August 18

David sits on the edge of the Peace Pond, dangling his feet in the water. "Are you here, Angela?"

"I AM, Davidlove. You seem deep in thought."

"Yes. Tomorrow is the first day back to school. I'm feeling excited and worried at the same time. I wonder if I will be able to keep my heart open when faced with teachers and kids judging me or when I start getting pushed around. I have had an incredible summer playing the Love Game with you, but I feel the real challenges are just ahead. Being in crowds of kids puts me on edge and tires me out. Will I get stomach aches like I have had before? Who will be my friend? Will my teacher like me, or will she scold me and humiliate me like my second-grade teacher did? Will I be bullied?"

"Wake up, Davidlove! You are creating a nightmare."

"What? I am awake."

"You were dreaming about unwanted things in the future that might make you feel bad. And it's no surprise that you made yourself feel bad right now. Your imagination was playing the survival game. Remember the last time you had a nightmare that woke you up with your heart pounding and muscles tense? Waking up gives you the opportunity to recognize that it was just a dream and allow your physical reactions to calm down. Waking up gives you the chance to come into the present moment, change your story, and create a perfect feeling."

"Even though I know that, I still find myself creating distress."

"That's a habit you have been practicing for a long time, Davidlove. Can you find a way to remind yourself that you can change your focus when you start feeling distressed?"

"Great idea. I'll let Peace Pond ponder that question for me."

"Angela, I'll tell you something that excited me today. Jeremy, in my Sunday School class, invited me to join his Boy Scout troop, which meets at the church. I really want to learn about camping and spend even more time in Nature. Jeremy tells me that they have a lot of fun together, including going to summer camp for a week."

"Nice shift in your energy, Davidlove. Now, what desire is bubbling up for you at this moment?

"I want to get on my bike and just ride."

"Where do you want to go?"

"To nowhere in particular."

"Davidlove, do you mean nowhere or now here?"

David laughs at the wordplay. "Love might say, there is nowhere to go because we are now here," she remarks.

"Angela, I want to get on my bike and ride, appreciating that I am already here at each moment. Maybe the bike knows the direction to go for the perfect adventure."

David gets on his bike and starts riding, and to his surprise, he finds himself outside Angela's house. "Angela, did you lead me here?"

"Not me, Davidlove."

"Since I'm here, I'll say hi to Nana, Rachel, and Sammy." David rings the bell, and Nana answers.

228

"What a wonderful surprise," she says, giving David a hug. "Rachel and I were just talking about you a few minutes ago." Rachel enters the room with a big smile. "I am so glad you stopped by, David." When they hug, David feels an electric energy surge through him. "Wow, Rachel, I not only see the Love you are, I felt it throughout my body."

"Thank you, David. I felt something special too. Come in and sit for a bit. Nana and I have something for you."

Nana comes in holding a small cloth bag with handles. He recognizes it immediately as the one Angela kept her journal and pencils in. Nana hands it to him, "This is for you."

Tears well up in David's eyes as he reaches in and pulls out Angela's sketchbook. On the front is written, "My Perfect Love Story." He turns the book over, and on the back are words, "WAKE UP DAVIDLOVE!" printed with a big red heart. He holds the book to his chest. "Thank you, Angela."

David looks deep into Nana and Rachel's eyes. "Thank you so much for this precious gift. It means a lot to me. Love is here."

"We both thought Angela meant for this to be yours. Have you been with Angela lately?"

"We talk with each other every day. I miss her touch," David says. "It makes me happy to imagine her looking into my eyes, kissing and hugging me. How about you guys?"

"I have frequent dreams where she talks to me," Rachel says. "But I still miss her. She inspired me to enroll in the local community college to become a certified nursing assistant. Dr. Deera thought I would be an inspiration to patients in the behavioral health unit in the hospital. You never know; maybe I will continue with my training and become a psychiatric nurse or even a counselor. For now, I am working in the housekeeping department at the hospital."

"That sounds great, Rachel. I agree with Dr. Deera. Your experiences, as difficult as they have been, are gifts that will serve to ease the suffering of others."

Nana says, "I hear Angela's voice periodically through the day. She tells me she is here and sees the Love I am. I turn to see her and smile at the empty space. I miss her laughter."

"I AM here, everyone."

They all reply, "Yes!"

"I have the sudden urge to ride my bike over to Mrs. Deera's house," announces David.

Rachel, Nana, and David enjoy a group hug before he leaves.

"I hope you have fun playing the Love Game at school tomorrow. Best wishes David," says Nana.

"Thanks, I probably will. Angela says she will help me to remember to wake up if I forget to make myself happy. Bye everyone, see you later."

****

Mark and Crystal have been spending more time together since Angela's passing. They have also shared Sunday lunches with Amma. Amma and Crystal just finished doing the lunch dishes. Amma goes to the cookie jar, takes out eight chocolate chip cookies, and puts them on a plate. She then pours a cup of coffee for Mark, Crystal, and herself and then places a glass of milk in the empty place on the table.

"Who's the milk for?" asks Mark.

"I have a feeling that David might show up." It wasn't more than a few seconds later that the doorbell rang.

"I'll get it," says Mark.

David's eyes and mouth open wide when he sees that it is Dr. Deera answering the door. "Hello David, we have been expecting you."

"Hey, Dr. Deera, what a nice surprise."

They hug each other.

"How did you know I was coming? I just decided to come about 10 minutes ago," says David.

"Mom had a feeling."

They give each other a hug. "Please come into the kitchen, David."

David lights up again when he sees Dr. Welling. She greets him with a nice hug, too. "I am so happy to see you today, David," says Mrs. Deera. That perfect feeling shot up like a rocket when they looked into each other's eyes. "Please sit down and have some cookies and milk as we visit." David sits down and enjoys a cookie and sip of milk.

"I was at Angela's house with Nana and Rachel when I got a sudden urge to ride my bike over to see you, Mrs. Deera. I'm so glad I did because I also got to see you, Dr. Deera, and you too, Dr. Welling. I have something I want to share with you guys. I left it in my bike basket." David hurried back out the front door to where he parked his bike and retrieved Angela's journal bag. He shows them the gift that Nana and Rachel gave him. He opens the journal, and they all huddle to see the drawings.

Tears were flowing all around when they finished looking at the journal.

They all sat back down in silence, their hearts wide open to the intense feelings of Love's presence.

"I AM here," Angela says.

Hearing that, each one touches their heart and then grasps the person's hands next to them to form a circle around the table.

Mark breaks the silence, "What a beautiful journal creating a magnificent and perfect moment. I am blown away by her dreams, especially the ones in her final days. The drawing of me and Crystal holding hands with a caption. "Dr. Welling and Dr. Deera sharing their Love. This was drawn before we even started dating."

"Angela and I could tell when you two were together that you were hiding a desire to be more than colleagues. She thought if she drew you two together, it would happen."

Crystal says, "My heart opened up seeing the drawing of me holding the crystal. That day, when you, David, and Angela gifted me the crystal, was the first day I experienced that Perfect feeling of Love and Oneness. I thought that I knew what love was before then, but any previous feelings were dwarfed by the magnitude of what I experienced that day and many more times since Angela's passing.

"I like the drawing of us meeting Roy, says Mrs. Deera. It was a wonderful time when I first realized the profound impact of multiple open hearts focused on Love. I would have liked to have had more time with Roy. He awakened from a very troubled, guilt-laden past to find his Divine Loveself. On that final day of his life, he connected to Love in a way that he thought was impossible. It gave me much hope."

David says, "All the drawings touch me, but the one that lifts my spirit the most and reminds me of our Divine Connection is the one she drew of us standing naked and petting a deer in the forest. We took our clothes off without any shame to honor the Love and beauty of our physical creation.

"Thank you so much for sharing Angela's Love Story with us, David," says Mrs. Deera.

"It was my joy to share."

Angela responds, "This is not just my Love story; it is our One magnificent Love Story, and it is not over yet."

David rides home feeling more confident than ever that he can create happiness by playing the Love Game at school tomorrow. It's going to be a marvelous adventure with lots of gifts.

Acknowledgments

Thanks to Francine Brevetti for your help editing this book. Your questions, perspective, experience, your willingness to communicate with me honestly and to go the extra mile was just what I needed to complete this book.

Thanks to Rodney Hatfield, who helped me navigate the world of marketing and give the book the best chance for being seen.

Thanks to Amayra Hamilton, Jane Baniewicz, Ann Bauden, John-Geo Stebila, Eveline Horelle Dailey, Larry Rosenberg and Amy Katz for reading the early drafts and offering loving perspectives and wisdom.

Thanks to my son, Jonathan, a writer himself, who encouraged me to follow the voice of my heart and not to worry about conforming to all the conventional writing rules.

Thanks to my son, Nathaniel, who was present anytime I felt stuck or down about the book. He supported me with a positive light-hearted presence which left me hopeful and smiling.

And thanks to my wife, Jane, who gives me the space, time and support during extended periods sitting in front of the computer writing.

About the Author

David Montgomery, M.D., is the author of *Loving to Heal: Easing the Way to Wellness.* A board-certified physician specializing in obstetrics and gynecology, David now enjoys a more generalized practice that holistically assesses the health of men and women in the comfort of their own homes.

Guided by his heart – whether in practicing medicine, painting, sculpting, writing, or even landscaping – he dedicates his life to healing and creativity.

Embracing the spontaneous nature of inspiration, David allows insights to emerge in the present moment from his Divine Loveself, resulting in a process full of mystery. His art reflects his values and spiritual journey. He lives with his family amidst the expansive beauty of Arizona.

Explore other works by David Montgomery, M.D.

Loving to Heal
Easing the Way to Wellness

Are you yearning to care for yourself and others from a more authentic, powerful place?

Loving to Heal reveals a transformative truth: genuine caring flows from opening your heart to the Divine Love within. This guide is for compassionate souls who sense there's a more impactful way to care; as healthcare professionals, parents, or natural nurturers in any role.

Through gentle guidance you will discover:
- How to open your heart to the Divine Love that sustains and nourishes
- Seven practical approaches to align your caring with this inner wisdom
- How to transform fear-focused fixing into Love-centered caring

This isn't about rigid rules or guilt-inducing 'shoulds.' It's an invitation to discover the sacred dimension of caring. Moment by moment, as you open to Divine Love, you'll transcend fear and embody the presence that naturally facilitates healing.

Don't let another day pass feeling disconnected from your divine source. Transform your caring journey now with *Loving to Heal* - because true healing begins with aligning with the Divine Love within."